FROM THE HEART

FROM THE HEART

MY AUTOBIOGRAPHY

SANDY CLARK

WITH SCOTT BURNS

BLACK & WHITE PUBLISHING

First published 2012
by Black & White Publishing Ltd
29 Ocean Drive, Edinburgh EH6 6JL

1 3 5 7 9 10 8 6 4 2   12 13 14 15

ISBN: 978 1 84502 418 5

A CIP catalogue record for this book is available
from the British Library.

Typeset by Ellipsis Digital Ltd, Glasgow
Printed and bound by Scandbook AB, Sweden

To Liz, Suzi, Gary and Nicky.
Thank you for being my dream team.

CONTENTS

CONTENTS

ACKNOWLEDGEMENTS

Sandy Clark and Scott Burns would like to thank Barry Anderson, Stuart Darroch, Ian Dawson, Craig Halkett, Craig Levein, Eric McCowat, Andy McInnes, Bill Smith, Scott Struthers, Willie Vass, Mike Murphy and the *Scottish Daily Express* for their help and assistance in the publishing process.

Scott would also like to thank Liz for the endless cups of tea and hospitality in his get-togethers in the Clark household. He would also like to just say thanks to his wife, Amanda, and sons, Ross and Aaron, for their help, support and patience along the way.

We would also both like to say thank you to Black & White for putting their faith in the project and making this book become reality.

FOREWORD
BY CRAIG LEVEIN

FIRST AND foremost, I have to say, it was a privilege and a pleasure to have played in the same Hearts team as Sandy Clark and then to work with him again when he became my manager at Tynecastle. He was a fearsome striker and a top coach and somebody I have always looked up to.

I'll start by talking about Sandy's playing career. He was absolutely fearless and always went in where it hurt, Sandy's all-action play was an inspiration to everyone around him. He was always up for a physical challenge and those flying elbows must have been a really frightening proposition for any central defender who was brave enough to face up to him. I am just glad he played the majority of his career with Hearts and I didn't have to come up against him directly, because I know he could have cost me my good looks!

Back then men had to be men. You had to win your individual battles and Sandy rarely came off second best. Thinking back, some of the aerial charges he made still make me shudder. There was a game against Rangers where Sandy and Craig Paterson clashed heads. There was blood everywhere and it was an absolutely horrendous sight. Both players got carted off but the next thing we knew Sandy was up on his feet, even though there was blood all over him, trying to get back on. A collision like that these days would see a player hospitalised for days but, at times, Sandy seemed almost indestructible. Back when we played you couldn't show people you were hurt because it was a sign of weakness and Sandy just epitomised that.

I joked a bit about his physical attributes but you can't take away from Sandy that he was also a very good footballer. He had a deft touch, decent pace and an eye for goal. I am in no doubt the current Hearts team would love to have somebody like Sandy leading the line for them.

As a defender, it was great to have Sandy in the team because he always gave us an out-ball. If you fired it up into Sandy's direction, even if it was a poor pass, you knew he could turn it into something. I know a lot of times people said to me that was a great pass out of defence, and I then had to hold up my hands and say, 'No, it wasn't, it was just a panicked clearance up the park. It was Sandy who produced the magic.'

Sandy also had a huge influence on the rest of the team. Many of us were still relatively young men, still making our way in the game. Sandy was a lot more experienced and an important cog in the wheel for our Hearts teams.

John Robertson is one of the most successful strikers that Hearts has ever had but he definitely owes a lot of that to Sandy Clark. Sandy was probably the single biggest influence on Wee Robbo's career. John is a Hearts legend but a lot of his achievements, especially in those early years, were down to Sandy. As an older player, I know Sandy passed a lot of advice on to John. He also took a lot of the knocks and dunts for John on the pitch. You only have to look at John's face today – he hardly has a mark, while Sandy's forehead is like a game of knots and crosses with all the scars and stitches he has collected in his career.

Sandy went on to become my manager at Hearts. Again, I really enjoyed working under him. He gave me and the rest of the other senior boys a lot more responsibility. It was something we never got under Joe Jordan and I think all the more experienced players, including myself, really thrived, again thanks to Sandy. He was a manager you wanted to play for and I really enjoyed working for him. I firmly believe that if he had been given more time then he would definitely have taken Hearts places.

It was a difficult season for the club when he inherited the job. Hearts were very much in a transitional period. We started poorly, but in the second half of the season our record was one of the best in the league. We had a fantastic finish and ended staying up and finishing well up the table.

There had been talk all that season that Wallace Mercer was going to be selling the club to Chris Robinson. I remember, as captain, I held a meeting with all the players and we were all in total agreement that we wanted Sandy to stay, although there were strong rumours that Robinson wanted to bring in his own manager. I went to speak to Chris and pleaded with him to keep Sandy. I was in no doubt the club was going in the right direction and Sandy had done a brilliant job at the end of that previous season. But during those initial discussions with Chris I knew he had already made his decision to appoint another manager. He never said anything but I could see in his eyes and in his actions that he wanted to replace Sandy and it didn't matter what any of us said or did. As the owner of the football club, he was perfectly entitled to make that decision although I felt, and I still feel, Chris made a mistake by sacking Sandy and replacing him with Tommy McLean.

Credit to Sandy, he picked himself up and went on to have further success with Hamilton and St Johnstone. I always felt he was destined to go on and become a top, top manager. You only have to look at his record. He has done well wherever he has been and that shows the managerial qualities he has. He is an honest and up-front guy and as a player that is all you can ask for.

I have learned from all the managers I have played under. A lot of the time it has been negative things and what not to do in certain circumstances, but what I can say about Sandy is nothing but positives. He treated me and the other senior players well and gave us the respect we never got from his predecessor, Joe Jordan. Sandy came in and got the senior players back on side and that, for me, showed good management. Sandy has always been a real people person, so approachable and easy to work for.

Even when he left Hamilton I know he put in a good word for me when he went to St Johnstone. I didn't get the Accies job but I appreciated Sandy putting my name forward. As I have said, Sandy has been a big influence on my own football career. So writing the foreword for this book is the least I can do to say thank you for everything Sandy has done for me.

Craig Levein

1

DIAMONDS ARE FOREVER

LEEDS UNITED or Airdrieonians? Let me put it another way. Join one of the giants of the British game, who had just lost their championship crown to Everton but were on the verge of going on to lift the Inter-Cities Fairs Cup for a second time under the legendary Don Revie, or pull on the white and red diamond of my hometown team, who had just finished twelfth in Scotland's own top league? That was the big decision I had to make when I was offered schoolboy forms by both.

There was only ever going to be one winner for this budding youngster that went by the name of Alexander Clark. Today most kids would give their right arm for the chance to play football in the English Premier League. They have been brought up on a diet of Sky Sports and the riches of Manchester City, Manchester United, Chelsea, Arsenal and Liverpool, but back then I was a boy of more humble taste. My footballing Mecca was Broomfield – the home of my beloved Airdrieonians. That love affair had been nurtured from an early age and by the time I had signed S-Forms I was a regular on the Airdrieonians Supporters Bus. Every Saturday and midweek this youngster from Dunrobin Primary School would set off on his weekly pilgrimage to watch his heroes, Derek Whiteford, Billy McPheat, Davie Marshall and Jim Black, in action. To get the chance to follow in their footsteps was a real boyhood dream come true and not even the pull of joining the mighty Leeds United was going to derail that. Airdrieonians or Airdrie United, as they are known today, have and always will be my team.

The Lanarkshire town is where I made my debut appearance to the world on 28 October 1956, the middle child of Robert and Margaret Clark. I joined the ever-increasing Clark clan, starting with my older sister Mary, and a few years later we greeted our younger brother Kenny. From an early age, people always said there was a real sporting talent within the Clark household. Unfortunately, they weren't talking about me because in those formative years I was left hovering in the shadows of Mary. She was a promising athlete and a really good runner – some people said she was even a better footballer than Kenny or myself. I am not one to argue, although if Mary was then it wasn't through a lack of practice on my part. I was out on the streets every spare minute, kicking a ball and dreaming of being the next Billy McPheat or Davie Marshall. Those eight-a-side kickabouts were where it all started for me, running about with my pals, on any bit of free grass, but more often than not we found ourselves playing in the street, Petersburn Road, using the driveway gates as goals. I can look back now and laugh because our games were a non-stop football marathon. We would go in for our tea or our lunch and then come back out and the same game would still be on-going. Ironically, the street actually backs on to the end of where the New Broomfield Stadium is today.

It wasn't until I started at Dunrobin Primary School that I got my first taste of organised football. Our school janitor, Mr Rooney, arranged trials for the school football team when I was in Primary Five. I remember it well because we won 6–0 and I scored four goals. Thankfully, that was enough to get me into the team –

even though I was by far the youngest, the rest of the guys were all a couple of years older than me. My first game for Dunrobin was also a memorable one because it was a local derby against our big rivals Clarkston. I couldn't have asked for a better start because we won 7–1 and I scored another four goals. We competed in the Airdrie Schools Cup, the oldest football tournament of its type in the world. That was a big thing for me. Although Dunrobin never really came close to winning it, it did give me my first taste of competitive football.

I moved on to Airdrie High but after a year up there I switched to a brand new purpose-built school called Caldervale High. It was there my football really kicked off, as we gained a bit of success through our school team. There were two teachers there who went on to have a big influence on my early career. One was Johnny Cross, today he would be classed as a guidance teacher but back then he looked after the so-called wayward kids. He would, quite literally, knock the rough edges off them and everybody else who stepped out of line. Mr Cross was a good sportsperson and a great football man but his main role in the school was maintaining discipline and he did it very successfully with half a cricket bat and his boot. I wasn't too bad. I think I only got a kick once (or maybe twice)! I was one of the lucky ones. Such physical discipline wouldn't be tolerated these days, but it kept everyone in line, even the worst offenders at the school had enormous respect for Mr Cross.

The other main influence on me was Peter Russell, who was a Physical Education teacher. He took the school football team and managed us with great success, as we won the Scottish Cup at under-14s and under-15s. To win the competition, at two different age groups, in successive years was an unbelievable achievement. I was in second year and then in third year when we won the competition. In both finals we played against St

Mungo's High School of Falkirk, they were both two-legged affairs. Strangely enough, we lost both first legs before we came back in the return to lift both trophies. In the under-14 final we lost 2–1 at home before we won 3–1 at Stenhousemuir's old Ochilview ground. The following year we lost 2–1 at Falkirk's Brockville and then won the second leg, quite convincingly 6–1, at Cliftonhill, the home of Albion Rovers.

One of the most famous guys I came across in those early years was Gordon Strachan. We faced his team, Edinburgh's Craigroyston High School, in one of the early rounds. You could see he had real ability, he stood out in his team and it wasn't just because of his ginger hair. Unfortunately, for him, he was on a hiding to nothing that day because we beat his Craigroyston team 7–3.

Our Caldervale team was almost unbeatable at our age group and not surprisingly there was a lot of interest from a number of clubs in our players. That was at the time when Leeds tried to sign me and a few others from the team, although by that point I already knew Airdrie were on the case. The local Airdrie scout had obviously been attracted by our Scottish Cup success and had approached the school and said he wanted to speak to me and my parents about signing S-Forms. I didn't need much persuading and I signed my S-Forms with Airdrie on 1 October 1970. It was the time when Ralph Collins was the manager and it was in the middle of a very successful spell for the Diamonds. They got to the final of the Texaco Cup a couple of years later and had a very good, competitive team. It was an exciting time for me and a lot of my teammates.

The captain of our Caldervale team, George Hunter, signed for Rangers as a kid but didn't really make it there and went on to play for Hamilton and Cowdenbeath before a back injury curtailed his career at a relatively young age. Our centre back,

Bobby Aitken, also went on to play for Hibs before he dropped down into the lower leagues. Norrie Anderson signed at Airdrie with me and together we came through the ranks. Norrie eventually took over the captain's armband from me when I left Airdrie. All in all it wasn't a bad return from one school team. The only mystery to me was that one or two more didn't actually enter the professional grade because the talent was certainly there.

I have always been an Airdrie fan. My first Airdrie team I still remember well; it was Roddy McKenzie, Paul Jonquin, Jackie Keenan, Bobby Ramsay, Jim Black, Derek Whiteford and Billy Wilson, along with two massive strikers in Billy McPheat and Davie Marshall, who were absolute beasts. Early on there was Drew Jarvie and Drew Busby, who were a great partnership. There was also John Phillips, a winger, and Willie McCulloch, who I ended up being teammates with when I later turned professional.

I used to go to every Airdrie game as a supporter. I didn't miss a match, home or away, and that started when I was eight or nine. There was an old wire fence at Broomfield beside the railway line I used to climb over to get in because at that time we didn't have a lot of money. It was either that or somebody would lift me over the turnstiles. It was great because that was back in the days before segregation and you could go right round the ground and change ends at half-time. I could go anywhere apart from the main stand because I couldn't afford to go up there. I also went on the Airdrie Supporters Bus myself, just to go and watch my beloved Diamonds. I got to know a lot of the boys on the bus and built up a lot of friendships. I am a born and bred Airdrie fan but I think when you are brought up in somewhere like Lanarkshire you tend to have an allegiance to one side of the Old Firm. That was the way it was back then and my other team was Rangers. I liked to keep an eye on their results as well and I also went to watch a few of their games when I was at secondary school. George Hunter stayed nearby me in Chapelhall and I sometimes used to travel through to Ibrox with him. It was only occasionally because if Airdrie were playing then I would always go and watch them, ahead of anybody else.

To get the chance to play for my beloved Diamonds was something I had always dreamed of. First and foremost, I had to sign my S-Form. It was a relatively straightforward process. I went down to Broomfield and put pen to paper. My dad got the signing-on fee – a couple of wee whiskies, so that was a bonus for him. I still had to play for the school team on a Saturday morning and for Airdrie Boys Club again in the afternoon. We would play two matches a day most Saturdays but now you are not allowed to do that because of the fear of burnout amongst young players. It certainly didn't do me or any of my peers any harm.

It was quite funny because the Airdrie captain, Derek Whiteford, was also a Physical Education teacher and he ended up teaching at Caldervale. I would go and train with Airdrie at night and Derek would be my teammate and then the next morning he would be back to being my teacher again. It was a little strange. I wish I could say he gave me some preferential treatment but he was even tougher on me than the rest of the boys. In fact he made my life hell, although I have to say it was in a good way. He just wanted me to do things the right way and that, to be fair, helped stand me in good stead. He was a good example to all the kids.

We used to have an old guy, who was jack-of-all-trades, at Airdrie called Willie McLaughlin. When I signed my S-Form one of the perks of playing for Airdrie at the time was that every

Sunday, after a home game, we could go down and help Willie to clear the terraces and replace the divots on the pitch, and suchlike. My early memories about cleaning up Broomfield, like all old grounds of that time, are when we had to pick up a massive amount of beer cans and whisky and vodka bottles. You can't get a drink at a football ground now but back then the laws were a little more relaxed. It was a hard shift but we got five bob for it which helped to supplement our wages. If we were really lucky then Willie would allow us to do a wee training session on the pitch after we had finished our chores. That was my first contact with Willie and he really was an iconic figure at the club. Willie would look after the pitch, the ground and would do just about everything that was asked of him. He could turn his hand to almost anything, there were times when you would come back at lunch-time and he was doing some physio on some of the injured players. The work was non-stop for Willie and he ended up taking on a young apprentice, who had just left school, called John McGuire. John is still the groundsman at New Broomfield today.

I longed for the day when I would get to grace the Broomfield turf. I eventually signed my professional forms with Airdrie in 1974 after I left school at seventeen. I sat my O Grades and got six out of six, I then went back to do my Highers but by that time I had started to focus more on my football and it was too much of a distraction. We will leave it at that. When my wife, Liz, and I go out I tell everyone we have got five Highers between us. I just don't tell anybody that Liz has got all five. I now coach at Cumbernauld College and I have completed a Higher National Certificate and Higher National Diplomas in sports coaching. I have also passed an HNC in sports coaching and fitness, which is a higher level, so I can say I eventually got my grades, it only took the best part of forty years!

When I swapped the terraces for the playing staff, my mum and dad ended up taking my seat (and a few others as well) on the Airdrie Supporters Bus. They didn't drive and so ended up travelling the length and breadth of the country to watch their eldest son in action via the bus. Mary and my brother-in-law, Alex Cooper, also started travelling to the games. Sometimes my biggest worry on a Saturday wasn't the football but trying to scrounge and acquire as many tickets as I could for everyone on the supporters' bus. Supporting Airdrie really has since turned into a family affair. Even now, it has moved on to the next generation and my sister's sons are all Airdrie diehards and season ticket holders. It is good to see we have kept it in the family. We will all be Airdrie till we die!

2

DO YOU WANT TO COME TO CELTIC?

I WAS playing part-time at Airdrie and took a full-time job in the Bank of Scotland. I did all the different front-of-office tasks, like being a clerk, counting money and doing the ledgers. It was the most boring job ever, but it had to be done because most of the clubs in Scotland around that time were part-time. My first professional contract with Airdrie was £12 a week, with another £8 if I was in the first-team squad. There was another £4 if I played and a further £10 bonus for a win or £5 for a draw. We also received another £5-a-point come the end of the season. It might not sound like much in today's terms but it was a lot of money back then. Even so I was still earning more from the bank than from football. My bank manager was an old gentleman called Hugh Swan. He was a great old man and retired not long after I took up my job, but I am assured it had absolutely nothing to do with my arrival. Mr Swan was really accommodating, he always allowed me to get away early for training or games.

Ian McMillan was the Airdrie manager when I turned professional. He had been the youth coach under Ralph Collins and had taken the under-18s when I had started to come through. Bobby Morrison was his Reserve team coach. Ian and Bobby were both good football people and wanted to help people better themselves in the game. I started playing in the second XI which was normally a reverse of the first-team fixtures, so if Airdrie were playing Dundee at home then the reserves would have a game up at Dens Park. When it came to football and getting a grounding then Airdrie was as good as you could have got. I was played in the second string with guys like Joe Hutchinson, Jim March, Norrie Anderson and John Jones, who ironically went to school with a certain Jimmy Calderwood and they still remain friends today. It was a good way to break you in.

There was also another young hopeful at Broomfield who went by the name of James Traynor. He was a full back, a local boy and Airdrie fan like myself. He went to the same school, although he was a good few years older than me. Jim had also been the captain of Caldervale High School. He never made it as a professional footballer but he certainly went on to make a name for himself in sports journalism. I have a lot of respect for Jim, I know he likes to be controversial but that is his job, and he certainly knows what is going on in football. He is also a genuine football person – although his claim to fame is the fact he says he played for Airdrie, I work with him regularly on BBC Radio Scotland and I always wind him up by saying, 'What do *you* know? You only played three games for Airdrie reserves!' He turned out as a trialist but never signed professionally. He was really enthusiastic and you could say he was competitive, to say the least. I hate to say it but he actually was a good player. Jim gave it absolutely everything and, like today, he never took prisoners, if Jim caught you with a tackle then you knew you would be struggling to get up again. Ultimately he was probably a little bit unfortunate not to get a contract with Airdrie.

Breaking into the team I also got to play alongside one of my heroes, Willie McCulloch. I loved his all-action style that made him such a terracing favourite at Broomfield. If you ever wanted to see commitment and effort then Willie was your man. He was a player who gave absolutely everything for the team and, as a player, somebody you wanted to have out there alongside you. Another legendary figure was Paul Jonquin, an Airdrie stalwart and a great full back into the bargain, and my teacher Derek Whiteford. There were also players like Jim March, Billy Wilson and Jim Black, all real Airdrie stalwarts.

My first involvement with the Airdrie first team was as a substitute. Norrie Anderson and I were both named on the bench in a game at Broomfield against Rangers. It was around Christmas of 1974 and Airdrie won an epic encounter 4–3. We didn't get on but we did pocket the win bonus, I think I walked away with another £40 without having to kick a ball. The reason I remember is because we used to get our wages in brown envelopes and when I had this extra money in it, I felt like a millionaire. I remember I took a £20 note out to pay for my driving lesson even though it was only £3 or £4. My driving instructor, Hughie Dunlop, whose own dad used to drive the Airdrie team bus, just looked at me as if I was mad because £20 was a small fortune back then. My top team debut came at Dens Park a few days before the turn of the New Year. I came off the bench and it was hardly a dream start because we lost 1–0 to Dundee. Tommy Gemmell and Jimmy Johnstone both played for Dundee, so to say I made my professional debut against two Lisbon Lions was special. I then had to remain patient. I made one more substitute appearance before I got my first start in a 3–1 win over Partick Thistle, with Derek Whiteford stealing the headlines with a hat-trick.

Airdrie got to the Scottish Cup final at the end of that 1974–75 season. It was a great achievement for the club and that team, quite rightly, is still heralded by the Airdrie support, as their heroes eventually went down bravely to a 3–1 defeat to Celtic. I played nothing but a support role in that run, where I was an unused substitute in an early round away to Morton. I was still at Hampden as a fan and I was cheering the team on with the rest of the diehards. It was disappointing we didn't go all the way but it was still a great occasion for the team, the club and the town. Getting to the final brought a real feel-good factor to Airdrie. That success also made me even more determined to force myself into the team. In the summer of 1975 the decision was taken to reconstruct the leagues. Instead of two leagues they switched it to three and, as a result, we went from the top league down to the Second Division. It was a disappointment but it worked in my favour and helped give me my chance.

I didn't have to wait long to make an impression, as I came off the bench against Dunfermline at East End Park in the following season, 1975–76, to score my first senior goal. I netted in a 3–3 draw and I also managed to set one up for Billy Wilson, so I was relatively pleased with my afternoon's work.

My first hat-trick came a couple of games later in a thumping 7–1 win at Queen of the South. Paul Jonquin was our penalty taker but I had scored twice and we were up 6–1 so he agreed to step aside to let me seal my hat-trick. Allan Ball was the Queen's goalkeeper. He is somebody I still bump into and I always wind him up that he couldn't have been that good because I scored my first senior hat-trick against him. I netted a few hat-tricks for Airdrie but I never got a match ball because the clubs couldn't afford to give them away. Money really was that tight.

From around Christmas I was either in the team or a substitute, so I got a lot of first-team experience in a short space of time. I finished that first full season with seven league goals, finishing one behind our top scorer Derek Whiteford. The team finished seventh in the Second Division although they went on to win the Spring Cup at the end of the season, beating Clydebank 4–2 after extra-time at Firhill. My part in that was pretty much limited to a watching brief. It was around that time Jackie Stewart replaced Ian McMillan as manager. I didn't play as much under Jackie, as he obviously didn't have as much confidence in me as Ian. I still managed to pitch in with seven goals in the league as the team finished sixth in the First Division. To be fair, there were signs of progress, like when we pulled Celtic in the Scottish Cup and drew 1–1 with them at Broomfield before we were taught a lesson in the second game when we were thrashed 5–0 at Celtic Park.

The following 1976–77 season I managed to break into double figures with my goals but we struggled to tenth and were closer to the drop zone than the promotion slots. The next season saw me sent off for the first time in my career. I only got red-carded once for Airdrie and it came on 7 October 1977 at Broomfield. I learned a lesson that day that I will never forget, I had scored to put us 1–0 ahead. I then got booked for gesturing to a linesman and five minutes later I made a stupid tackle, which left the referee with little option but to book me again and send me off. We ended up getting beat 2–1. I was back in the dressing room and I will never forget when the door crashed open and big Jim Black walked in. He was a great, great professional but he was as hard as nails – he used to work on a machine call The Grip. It was used to help lay roads and Jim had hands like shovels. He came right up to me and I just saw this big hand go up into the air, I thought: Oh no! I feared the worst because if he had swung at me he would have killed me. I saw the anger in his eyes. Thankfully he only threatened me but that was more than enough to get the message across. He said: 'You f***** cost me money this weekend.' I then realised what I had done, I had let myself, my team and the fans down. I realised how stupid I had been.

My fortunes changed for the better when Bobby Watson replaced Jackie Stewart at the Broomfield helm. It was probably the best thing that happened to me and it turned out to be the most successful spell of my Airdrie career. Bobby came in and pretty soon after he asked me to become captain. I seemed to thrive under the extra responsibility. I was playing up front with Willie McGuire, we struck up a decent understanding and scored a lot of goals together. We had a good partnership and it was pretty much the classic big guy-little guy partnership: I was the one who would offer a physical presence and Willie would offer the movement and speed alongside me. We worked well together and we finished sixth in the Second Division in that 1978–79 season. I also ended up as the club's top scorer with twenty-three league goals, so there was progress on all fronts, as a team and individually, and that was down to Bobby Watson's guidance. I was getting a bit older and more mature and I was becoming more aware of my strengths and weaknesses and my fitness.

By that time I had left the bank. I went to work for the Provident, a credit company. I had a decent job working in Glasgow, with a good bit of responsibility, so financially going somewhere full-time wouldn't really have been feasible. I also continued to get some good press on the back of that 1978–79 season. There were a few clubs who had started to sit up and take notice, which was flattering. Hibs tried to buy me when Eddie Turnbull was the manager; Airdrie turned down a bid of £160,000 from the Easter Road outfit. I knew Celtic also had an interest, I found out because Jimmy Steele, who was the masseur to Jock Stein's great Celtic team, had a company who supplied a lot of goods to the Provident and I got to know Jimmy through that. To say he was a character is an understatement, he always came in larger than life and would start kicking stuff about the office and try to get me to play football. I still remember the day he came in and said, 'Do you want to come to Celtic? Big Billy

[McNeill] wants to sign you.' My response was, 'Oh, does he?' That was all I said. I never did give him an answer. In the end, it never really came to me having to make a decision because I was never told officially about Celtic's move from anybody at Airdrie. A few years later, Billy McNeill, the manager then, confirmed he had tried to sign me. I know I might have been lambasted by quite a few of my friends if I had gone to Celtic, but, in the end, it never came to pass.

3

THE TON-UP KID HITS THE
BIG-TIME – EVEN IF I
EVADED FERGIE!

THERE WAS a genuine belief that we could use the 1979–80 season to make a real push for promotion to the Scottish Premier Division. Hearts and Motherwell, our big Lanarkshire rivals, had just been relegated and were the teams who were being tipped to battle it out for the title. Hearts, however, were by far the big fish and the side we all had to try and beat. We didn't really start the season particularly well but we eventually got into our stride and by the October we had pushed ourselves to the top of the pile. We also showed we could compete with the best – drawing 2–2 with Hearts at Tynecastle and then thrashing Motherwell 4–0, where I managed to get on the scoresheet. That 'Well side certainly weren't as intimidating as many of their predecessors. It was always interesting when we played Motherwell, especially when I was breaking through at Airdrie. There was the local rivalry but there was also a bit of added spice to the derby. We labelled them 'The Crazy Gang' long before Wimbledon took copyright to that unflattering label. It was down to guys like Gregor Stevens, who was later to become my teammate at Rangers; Willie Watson; Stewart McLaren, who I would go on to play with at Hearts; and Peter Millar. Willie McVie, their centre half, was another one. They were mad, the hardest group of players I probably came across in all my time in football. Motherwell were a real hardy bunch. McVie eventually moved on to Hearts and I remember I took my long-awaited revenge on him later on in my Airdrie career. Let's just say I didn't miss him. It was in those pre-shin pads days and he ended up with quite a bad cut down his shin. I just thought, 'That is one back for all the times you battered me about.' At Airdrie you learned how to look after yourself.

We were never out of the top three with Ayr and Dumbarton also up there challenging Hearts and ourselves. We hit the top in March again with a win at Ayr United and we eventually went on to clinch promotion against Motherwell at Broomfield. It came on 19 April when we won 3–1 and I scored a really good goal from a tight angle past Hugh Sproat, as Gordon Hamilton and Jim Rodger also got on the scoresheet. Winning promotion against Motherwell was great, especially for the fans because they were one of our main rivals and there was a big crowd that day to see us get over the line. We had won promotion but still had a chance of going up as champions which came down to a final day decider at Tynecastle. A draw would have been enough to see us crowned champions but Hearts beat us 1–0 to pip us at the post. Hearts probably deserved to win it. Looking back I wish there had been a role reversal that season, where Airdrie would have won the league and Hearts would have won the Scottish Premier Division title in the 1985–86 season, but it wasn't to be and I missed out on two championship medals.

On a personal note, I was pretty pleased with the way the season had gone. I scored twenty-one goals in the league and I was named as the First Division player of the year. It was pleasing but I would have much preferred to end the season with the championship trophy in my hands. For the team, it was a big disappointment not to come out on top but it was still a great achievement to win promotion. It had been a season of hard work. That along with our team spirit helped us achieve what we did that season. We had a real unity and that was because we all got on well together and socialised a lot. There were a few of us who liked a pint or two. Guys like Willie McCulloch, John Lapsley, Jim Black, Willie McGuire, Ian Gordon, Norrie Anderson and Brian McKeown all enjoyed a little refreshment in some of the town's local establishments like The Double A or Diamonds, that were owned by the former Airdrie player Billy Wilson. My local was always The Tavern which was another of Billy's pubs.

It was also at the stage that I had started to settle down and I got married to my girlfriend, Anne Turner, in 1979. She was a local girl who I had been dating for the previous two years and Anne was probably my first serious partner. So it was all change for me on the home front and that took a bit of adjusting for both of us.

Football-wise, Airdrie were continually improving. We went up and survived in the Premier League, even though everybody had tipped us to drop right back down again. I managed to get a few goals and that was good for me because a lot of people had questioned if I could cut it at the highest level. I had scored goals in the First Division but could I do it against the best? I really didn't look at it that way. For me and the team, it was another challenge and we just wanted to give it our best shot. Confidence was high after our promotion and we managed to punch above our weight. Hearts ended up going straight back down, along with Kilmarnock, who I wasn't too upset at seeing go down. There was a game at Rugby Park where my own supporters' club almost caused a riot. I had turned round and a Kilmarnock fan launched a pie at me, but he didn't realise my dad was standing next to him, with one of his mates, Bob Davidson, who worked with him at British Steel. The Killie supporter picked the wrong Airdrie player at the wrong time. Big Bob was built like the side of a mountain, he was a giant of a man and a champion caber tosser into the bargain. Bob just grabbed the man by the neck and I thought he was going to kill him. He ended up giving him the fright of his life and the guy realised that a pie thrower was going to be no match for a caber-tossing champion.

That season my Airdrie team also managed to hit the heights, finishing a more than credible seventh. Again, we managed to safeguard our top-flight status quite early on so that lifted a lot of the pressure off us. It was an incredible achievement for a club the size of Airdrie, we really did well. If you look at some of the teams in the league that season, Partick Thistle, Morton, Kilmarnock and St Mirren, we were certainly on a par with a lot of them, although maybe we weren't the best of teams to watch. We were more a kick and rush team but we were certainly effective in what we did. You have to remember we were still only part-time, training twice a week. If you want to keep the fitness up then you need to do the heart and lung stuff. My memory of training at Airdrie was that ninety percent of the time was spent running round the ash track at Broomfield. Bobby's assistant, Wilson Humphreys, was renowned as a great coach and worked at St Mirren and Motherwell too. He would occasionally try to do a bit of shape and formation but those sessions were few and far between because we didn't have the time or the facilities. We just went out and played and gave it our all.

There is no doubt playing at Broomfield was another big advantage, it was an intimidating place to play for any opponent. When I later signed for Rangers, Peter McCloy, the goalkeeper, said to me, 'What about that place you used to play? The Bull Ring – Broomfield.' He said that because he knew when he had to play there he was in for one almighty battle. It was a wee, tight pitch and the crowd was right on your back, especially in the Main Stand. In the big games, the Old Firm and the Motherwell derbies, where the stadium was packed the Airdrie support was like a twelfth man – and I am not just saying that. It was definitely an intimidating arena and most of the time the players didn't let our supporters down.

The 1980–81 season was where I got my only Scotland recognition. I had finished as Airdrie's top scorer with ten goals and I was called up for the Scottish semi-professional team. Bill Munro, who later went on to manage me at Airdrie, took the team. It was basically the best players from Scotland's semi-professional clubs that played in a tournament over in Holland. I was the captain and the squad included my Airdrie teammate Willie McGuire and other top players like Gerry McCabe, Jim Fallon, Jim Gallacher and Eric Morris. It was also the first time I came across a youngster that went by the name of Ally McCoist, who was with St Johnstone. We had a good team and did pretty well in that tournament. I scored a hat-trick in our first game against England and we went from strength to strength and went on to win the competition which was great. The Scotland manager Jock Stein was also across and I had hoped to catch his eye but I never got the call. I would have loved to play for my country but we had such an abundance of top strikers at that time, guys like Kenny Dalglish and Joe Jordan amongst them. It was always going to be something of a long shot for me to get any sort of recognition at that level. There was always a lot of press speculation but it never really happened which is still a major source of disappointment because I was desperate to play for Scotland. I would go and play against Rangers and Celtic and do well against their defenders and it was the same against Aberdeen, who had Alex McLeish and Willie Miller, and Dundee United, who had Paul Hegarty and David Narey. Names and reputations weren't something that bothered me, I always felt I did well against better players, but it just wasn't to be for me on the Scotland front.

I might not have been in demand on the international scene but there was always a fair bit of interest in me domestically. Teams kept being linked with me although nothing ever seemed to come to fruition. Partick Thistle made an offer and I have to admit that the switch appealed to me because they were offering me a lot more money to play part-time but Airdrie blocked that. Alex Ferguson, before he became a Sir, tried to sign me for Aberdeen. I desperately wanted to go to Pittodrie. The previous season Aberdeen had won the league and were on the verge of something that looked really big – although even I didn't know how big at that point – as the Dons went on to dominate Scottish football and lift the European Cup Winners' Cup in 1983. Eventually Sir Alex had to give up because he couldn't get me out of Airdrie, it was frustrating but there was nothing I could do. I tried everything in my power to make it happen. It wasn't down to the manager, Bobby Watson, I know that. He would have been happy to see me go on and better myself but the board viewed things differently, they blocked my move because it didn't suit them. We had won promotion and managed to stay in the top flight and they obviously thought I could play a major part in keeping them up for a second season. The disappointing thing for me was they didn't give me or my career a second thought. It was long before the days of Bosman. Airdrie owned my registration and if they didn't agree to release me then I had to stay where I was. The ironic thing was that I never signed another professional contract with Airdrie after my first one. I didn't need to because the clubs could retain your contract for as long as they wanted. They might put your money up or give you extra bonuses but you didn't actually have to put pen to paper again. I have nothing but good memories of my time at Airdrie, although I was disappointed at that time that they wouldn't allow me to join Aberdeen. I did start to think, 'Am I going to get my move?' At least I knew about Aberdeen's bids. It wasn't until I moved to Hearts a good few years later, when I was looking through some archive stuff at Tynecastle, that I found out that Willie Ormond had also made a bid for me but nobody at Airdrie cracked a light about that.

At times the press would inform me about some of the interest. The likes of Jim Traynor and Andy McInnes, who I knew from Airdrie, were always willing to help and keep me in the loop if they stumbled upon speculation or snippets of information that might be of interest. There was also a young guy who went by the name of Craig Halkett. He was a local boy and he started to come to the games and take pictures as a bit of a hobby. To be fair, it worked out really well because Craig ended up getting a full-time job as a photographer with the local newspaper, the *Airdrie and Coatbridge Advertiser*. He covered hundreds of our games and went everywhere with us; Craig was almost part of the team. At the end of each season most of the boys would club together and try to get a wee end-of-season break somewhere. One summer we went out to Ibiza – that was before it became the hip, party island it is today – and Craig came out with us to cover the trip for the paper. But I now have to let the editor into a little secret. If you think your photographs were a bit sharper on that trip, that was because I took every single one of them. I had to, otherwise the *Airdrie and Coatbridge Advertiser* would have been left with a few blank pages. Craig was under the influence of alcohol from the moment he stepped foot in Ibiza until the moment he got back on the plane. He later went on to work for the *Daily Record* and I always tell him that it was my pictures on that trip that got him there.

I went into the 1981–82 campaign looking to try and build on our success of the previous season. We knew it would be a lot harder second time around and that proved to be the case. We were scoring goals for fun but were letting in even more at the other end. I scored doubles in our opening two games but we lost 5–2 at Celtic and then 4–3 at home to St Mirren. I scored a couple of goals to give us our first win of the season against Dundee United and got a hat-trick in our 4–2 win over Dundee, which temporarily took us out of the relegation places, but we quickly slipped back again. We gave ourselves a bit of hope at the turn of the year after we beat Partick Thistle at the end of the February but that slipped away. Bobby Watson ended up stepping down and Bill Munro took over. Bobby had a successful business outside of football and there were a few problems behind the scenes at Airdrie he was unhappy with. The board didn't share his vision to take the club forward and so I think they agreed that a mutual parting of the ways was best for both parties. I felt a bit aggrieved that Bobby had left the club because I had the utmost respect for him and I know I owed him a lot. I decided then and there that I wanted to go. I also have to be honest and say I gave Bill a bit of a hard time. I only played seven or eight games for him as that season drew to a close. I had decided it was time to go and probably from Bill's point of view it was also in his interests to move me on. I was maybe becoming too strong a character for him. We struggled and eventually we ended up getting relegated. We failed to win a game under Bill that season. I certainly didn't give anything less than 100 percent, I knew what it meant to play for the Airdrie shirt and I was also playing to try and get myself a move. The situation made me even more determined to do well and to try and catch somebody's eye. Airdrie finished bottom of the table, some eight points away from safety. We ended up going down with

Partick Thistle and it was a big disappointment although the writing had been on the wall over the final couple of months of the season.

I scored seventeen goals and my strike against Morton on February turned out to be my 100th goal for Airdrie. All in all I scored 101 goals for the Diamonds which wasn't a bad return from a young boy who had come through the ranks. I was pleased at how I had done but it meant nothing in the grand scheme of things knowing that Airdrie were heading back to the First Division. My disappointment was diluted a bit by the shock that I had been named as the Players' Player of the Year, which was amazing. I was really taken aback and honoured when I found out. That along with the writers' award is massive, but to get the trophy from your fellow professionals meant that bit more.

I think then Airdrie realised my stock was at its highest and it was time for them to cash in. I was twenty-five and I knew I was ready to go full-time. I had a really good job and I loved playing for Airdrie but I remember saying to myself, 'Will you regret things when you are thirty-five and you have never given full-time football a crack?' Thankfully it did happen. My final game for Airdrie came against Dundee on the last day of the 1981–82 season. I was given permission to speak to the West Ham United manager John Lyall after the match – that was the first I was made aware of their interest. It then transpired he had been at the game and had been watching me for a while. I ended up meeting John in the Park Hotel in Falkirk and signed for West Ham the next day. It was an easy decision. I was going to the top league in England and joining a club with a proud history and top pedigree. They had a string of top players and John really impressed me with his plans for me and the club. Everything was agreed very quickly and I shook hands on a deal of £425 a week, which was a lot more than I was earning in my two jobs, including playing for Airdrie. George Peat, who went on to become the President of the Scottish Football Association, was the secretary of Airdrie at the time when I was sold. I had just got the club £200,000 and I asked him if he was going to give me any of the transfer fee and he turned round and told me that I wasn't getting a penny. Believe me, he stuck to his word!

In all honesty, I was just pleased that Airdrie had got something back for me. They had invested a lot of time in me and had given me the platform I needed to move on. Without them and my teammates I would never have got my move to West Ham. I appreciate everything that Airdrie have done for my career and I will always remain a fan. I always follow their results and it despairs me to see where they have dropped to in recent seasons and to see what has happened to them financially. It was probably the right thing to do to sell the old Broomfield and progress the club, although things certainly weren't handled too well, as Airdrieonians eventually went to the wall. They have come back as Airdrie United now but I still see them as Airdrieonians – they will always be Airdrieonians to me. I had a few chances to go back but the timing just wasn't quite right. They wanted me to become player-manager when I was still at Hearts. What put me off was that I was only thirty and I was still playing in the Hearts first team. The Hearts manager, Alex MacDonald, told me Airdrie had been on but it didn't take me long to say no because I still wanted to focus on playing at that time, I still felt I was a bit young to go into management. When Gordon McQueen was manager of Airdrie he tried to sign me as a player, but I decided to stay at Hearts. Then when Alex MacDonald moved to Airdrie he tried to bring me in as his assistant manager. It didn't work out because the Hearts chairman Wallace Mercer was desperate to keep me. He sort of half-promised me a future crack at management with Hearts and to be fair to him that eventually happened. Certainly, I would love to go back to manage Airdrie one day. With my connections with the club and being an Airdrie fan I would love to be manager there before I call time on my football career. Airdrie are and will always be my team.

4

THE HAPPY HAMMER

I ALWAYS had a gut feeling, even when I was younger, that I would one day play in the English top flight. I was delighted that it came to fruition, it was an experience I will never forget. I was lucky enough to play for a big team like West Ham United and under a great manager in John Lyall. John just let me go out and play, I couldn't have asked for any more. He would talk about movement as a striker or where he would want you to be in a game but he would never impose things on you. He would just gradually get his point across and his methods were certainly effective. He had a lot of respect for his players and we all had great respect for him. Very rarely did he get angry or upset although when he did you knew about it. He could be volatile when he needed to be but that was always something of a rarity. His forte was as a talented tactician. Even the smallest of changes he made could make a big difference to the team and the final outcome of games. John had this great ability to read games and to exploit weaknesses in the opposition. It was like a sixth sense.

Personally, training full-time under John brought my game on in leaps and bounds. I remember Sir Alex Ferguson came down to watch West Ham games that season. He had obviously tried to sign me for Aberdeen but I don't think even Sir Alex would have fancied his chances of getting me to swap West Ham for

Pittodrie. He was friendly with John, who had invited him down to a midweek game. I did okay and Sir Alex did a rather flattering article in one of the Scottish newspapers after the game about me. He said he had seen a big difference in my play due to full-time coaching and the level I was now playing at. That was a big boost to my confidence.

When I arrived at West Ham it was like I had moved into a completely new world. Upton Park, or the Boleyn Ground as it is more formally known, was a great wee stadium, although it has changed quite a bit today. You could probably have compared the old Upton Park to the old bull ring at Broomfield. There was a big main stand but the rest of the ground was terracing. It made for a great atmosphere, especially when it came to the big clubs coming down or the London derbies. Most of the time the stadium was packed. The West Ham public certainly love their football and they like to see the game played in the right way, John's West Ham teams got the ball down and knew how to play. The fans appreciated that and got right behind us. It was an amazing feeling running out at Upton Park. Suddenly, I was playing in front of crowds of at least 30,000 every other week and it really was something special.

John Lyall greatly impressed me during that first pre-season. Working with John gave me my first inclination that I might want to go into coaching myself further down the line. West Ham was night and day to what I had been used to as a player with Airdrie. In fact, the next summer I started my coaching badges through the SFA, doing my B Licence. At Broomfield we didn't have the same time for training because we were only part-time, doing a couple of sessions a week.

Suddenly, I was at West Ham and we had our own training ground away from Upton Park with four or five magnificent pitches and an indoor training area. This was also back in 1982, so it just showed the facilities and the foresight that the people at West Ham had. Everything was there for you to better yourself and after I adjusted to the full-time training it was a great life; we would train in the morning and then have the afternoons to ourselves and we would also get another day off during the week as well. I wasn't used to having so much spare time because back at Airdrie I was always trying to juggle my football around my work. It took a bit of adjustment getting used to full-time football and life in London.

What worked in my favour was that I was a wee bit older when I made the move, twenty-five, so I was more mature than maybe I would have been if I had gone down there as a teenager. I was also never one to hit the nightclubs or the bright lights of the city. I loved a beer, I still do, but I would rather go to my local with my mates and have a quiet pint.

There was a good mix of players at West Ham. We all got on really well but I was probably closer to my fellow Scots, Ray Stewart, Neil Orr and my good friend George Cowie, who was only a young lad at the time. George and I later went on to play together again at Hearts. I also got on really well with the big Scouser Alvin Martin, who was a top defender, and the Belgian international Francois Van der Elst. Franky was a top-class player, West Ham had signed him from New York Cosmos, where he had played with Franz Beckenbauer and Pele, so his background was decent to say the least. He is the best player I have seen when one-on-one with the goalkeeper – he hardly ever missed, whether he went round the keeper, chipped him or put it through his legs. He was absolutely clinical in that situation.

Franky and I actually, just by chance, ended up as neighbours. We used to travel in together every day from our home village of Shenfield, near Brentwood, in Essex. We became good friends but he wasn't your typical footballer. His technique and talents were unbelievable but he also loved a beer and a cigarette into the bargain. We spent quite a few nights together in our local pub, The Eagle and Child, when I was down there. It was reasonably easy to settle in at West Ham and to my new life in England. They were a good club and the players and staff couldn't have been any friendlier to me. I know I was away from home but my family were down every other weekend for games, so that also made settling into my new surroundings that bit easier. I still have quite a lot of friends from my time down at West Ham, including Franky. He was a complete one-off.

I remember when Franky got the call-up from Belgium for the European Championship qualifier against Scotland back in 1982. The match was over in Belgium at the Heysel Stadium and he needed a lift to Heathrow Airport so he could fly out and join up with the rest of his international teammates. I agreed to drop him off and then I said I would pick him up when he returned a couple of days later. Anyway I sat down to watch the game and it was the match where Kenny Dalglish scored two absolutely unbelievable goals but unfortunately for Scotland Franky scored two, equally as good strikes to help Belgium win 3–2. I wasn't happy and I actually thought about just leaving Franky standing at the airport, forcing him to make his own way home. In the end, I relented and picked him up although I must admit I gave him a fair amount of stick on the journey back home. But it didn't bother him one bit. In fact, he just laughed and I got his usual response, 'Come on, let's go for a beer' and then everything was forgotten. That just summed Franky up – he was so easy-going.

I spent that first New Year in a hotel room with Franky – it wasn't through choice. We were in the team hotel at Hogmanay, preparing for our derby clash with Tottenham on New Year's Day. The Belgians, like ourselves, love to celebrate the New Year, so we stayed up and I gave him his first introduction to the real taste of Scotland at the bells – Tennent's Lager. I had sneaked a couple of cans in with my kitbag. We had a quick drink and then I phoned back to Scotland and Franky called his family in Belgium. The next morning I went round the breakfast table and shook everybody's hands. The rest of the English boys were just looking at me as if I was an idiot. I then found out that the English didn't celebrate New Year quite as vigorously as us Scots. In fact, I think they were all sound asleep when the bells came in. That was the one and only time I had a drink the night before a game, although it was always a different story after the final whistle. I loved to have a beer on a Saturday, after a long hard week on the training field.

Our New Year drink certainly didn't affect Franky or me on the pitch, as we both played well and helped West Ham to a convincing 3–0 win over Spurs. The star of the day, however, was a debutant who wasn't even old enough to drink. The Hammers legend-in-waiting Tony Cottee made his top-team bow as a fresh-faced seventeen-year-old. It is fair to say his career never looked back, as he went on to play for England and Everton before he returned for a second spell at Upton Park. Tony was a deadly goalscorer and went on to prove what a top player he was.

The good thing from my point of view was that I was playing in a top team, with a good blend of youth and experience. There were the guys I have already mentioned and we also had a string of England caps: Phil Parkes was our goalkeeper, Alvin, Sir Trevor Brooking, Billy 'Bonzo' Bonds, Frank Lampard (senior), Alan Devonshire and Paul Goddard, my strike partner, who was similar in style to John Robertson, my ex-Hearts side-kick. We had some unbelievable talent at West Ham during that period. It would probably surprise a lot of people but out of all the players I played with down there I would say Devonshire was the pick of the bunch; he had unbelievable talent. Alan played wide on the left-hand side but he was right-footed. He would cut inside all the time but he was a really graceful player, he was an absolute nightmare for every one of his opponents. They all probably knew he was going to cut inside but they still couldn't stop him.

Billy 'Bonzo' Bonds is a real West Ham legend. He would always lead from the front. He would take the long runs in pre-season training and would often leave the rest of us trailing in his huge shadow. He had such natural fitness and he drove everybody on and would never allow anyone to slack off. He had such high standards and, to be fair to him, he was as good in games as he was on the training field. The only time I saw him struggle in a game was when a young Cyrille Regis was at West Bromwich Albion. He was an absolute tank and he was the only guy I saw give 'Bonzo' a hard time physically. We still won the game won 2–1 but it was a real eye-opener seeing Billy come off second best for once. It was such a rarity because he was such a massive physical presence to the team.

There was also Geoff Pike and, up front, we had Goddard and Brooking and then Cottee who came into the team after his New Year bang. Trevor actually had a bad injury and missed a lot of that season. He was always an easy target when the abuse started flying in our dressing room for never being fit. The boys used to joke and call him a bit of a girl's blouse but when he did play everyone could see the obvious talent he had. Trevor, to be fair, would always just laugh off the stick and criticism.

I also used to kill myself laughing when our international players, like Brooking, Martin, Parkes, Goddard and Devonshire, used to come back from England duty. The late Sir Bobby Robson was the manager and he never used to be able to remember their names and kept calling them all the wrong ones – you would have Phil Martin and Alan Brooking. It was the same after every trip. The boys would come back and tell us all the tales, but if he couldn't remember names it certainly didn't affect him on the football pitch because he was one of the best managers the British game has ever seen.

We had a top team and at one stage we were challenging for the First Division title. I had chipped in with a few goals here and so it really was happy days. It was a complete culture change for me because Scottish football was like a goldfish bowl compared to the top flight in England. Anywhere we went we would travel the night before and we would stay in top hotels and get the best of food and everything to make life easy for us. It was certainly different from making a mad dash away from my day job to get ready for midweek games with Airdrie.

There were quite a few highlights from my time at West Ham, like scoring my first goal for the Hammers in a 5–0 win over Birmingham City and then going on to net four goals in my next three games. I also scored against Liverpool which was good, in a 3–1 win. We were doing really well in that spell and beat Manchester United 3–1 at home. We rose as high as second in the league and we were really flying, beating some big teams, including Tottenham Hotspur along the way. If I am being honest, we did believe there was a chance we could win the league, things were going that well. I also scored a tap-in from six yards to help us beat Norwich City in the November. The game was on television and after that win the belief really grew. We hadn't played that well against Norwich but we had ground out the result and that is what you need to do when you are chasing titles. We did put up a challenge for a wee bit but, in the end, we came up a bit short of the likes of Liverpool, who went on to win the league that season, ahead of teams like Watford, Manchester United, Nottingham Forest and Spurs.

My claim to shame that season was I ended up scoring the one and only own goal of my career, in the League Cup against Lincoln. The first leg at Lincoln ended 1–1. Then in the second game at Upton Park I managed to put Lincoln ahead. The ball hit off me and ended up in the back of our net. You can imagine the abuse I took after that game. Thankfully, I managed to score the winner in our 2–1 triumph at home to make up for that and put us through in the end which took some of the heat off me. I ended up netting ten goals in thirty-four games for West Ham, which I didn't feel was too bad a return for my first season in England, even though I didn't actually see the campaign out.

5

NO, SANDY WOULDN'T BE
INTERESTED IN JOINING RANGERS

I HAVE to hold my hands up and admit that I actually knew Rangers wanted to sign me before anyone at West Ham United was aware of the interest, officially or otherwise. It was the late journalist Ken Gallacher who made the first phone call to tell me the Ibrox giants were interested. A lot of the sounding out back then was done through the press. Ken came on and said, 'Would you fancy a move to Rangers?' It caught me totally by surprise and it took me a wee bit of time to weigh everything up and get my head round things. I had a lot to consider and was a bit taken aback because the news, quite literally, had come out of the blue. I was happy and more than content at West Ham but the lure of playing for Rangers was something that had always appealed to me. I knew in my heart of hearts that was where I wanted to go and so I said to Ken, 'Yes, maybe if something can be agreed between the two clubs.' A couple of days later John Lyall pulled me aside after training and said, 'Listen, we have had Rangers on the phone. They said they were interested in signing you. I told them that I didn't think you would want to go and I also said we didn't want to sell you.' I think John thought that would be the end of the matter until I replied, 'Well, I might.' I could see he was really surprised and taken aback. He was shocked because I was his top scorer at West

Ham. If I had seen out the season there then I think there would have been a fair chance I could have finished top of our goal-scoring charts. Paul Goddard ended up winning that award with twelve goals, while Ray Stewart and Frankie Van Der Elst finished one goal ahead of me. I was pleased with my goal return and I think the manager thought I was genuinely happy at Upton Park. I was but the chance to play for Rangers was just too big an opportunity to turn down. I certainly wouldn't have gone back to Scotland for any other team. I knew Rangers weren't a dominant force north of the border but they were still one of the biggest clubs, along with Celtic. They had been guilty of under-achieving but the potential of Rangers was absolutely massive. If they could get things right on the pitch then I was confident the club could really take off. They had also won a few cups and so I knew going to Rangers would give me the chance to finally land silverware. Then there was also the added incentive of getting the chance to play in European football. There were plenty of positives. I might have made a different decision today, with the massive gulf in finances between the English Premier League and the Scottish Premier League, but back then the wage structures were pretty comparable.

I think John quickly realised that I wanted to go and to be fair to him he said, 'We will go back to them and see what they are talking about in terms of the financial side of the deal.' John knew I was desperate to go and didn't want to block the opportunity, knowing he could end up with an unhappy player on his hands. In the end, it all worked out, which, obviously, I was pleased about. I know for a fact that my upbringing and coming from Airdrie made the pull of Rangers a big thing. I also felt that if I didn't grab the opportunity there and then it might not have come round again. If I hadn't gone to Rangers then I know I would have regretted it. It wasn't about the money, even when

John Greig came down to London to meet me for the first time I wasn't really bothered about the financial side of things. Money was important but it was always secondary to my football. I actually ended up taking a fairly sizable wage drop to push the deal through. I got a signing-on fee from Rangers, which helped, but I still had to take a major hit. I think I dropped down to £300 a week, that was the basic wage everyone at Ibrox was on at that time. My decision to return to Scotland wasn't taken lightly or on a whim. If you looked at the hard facts I would have probably been better staying at West Ham but nobody could ever argue how big a club Rangers are. There is a real history and aura about the Glasgow giants and I knew from playing against Rangers just how big they were. Thankfully, West Ham got back the majority of the money they paid Airdrie and I got my move back up the road. It left everybody satisfied, even if John Lyall, maybe, wasn't as happy as me.

There is no point in looking back in life but I do wish my Rangers switch had happened two or three years further down the line. I have very few regrets from my time in football but the fact I didn't stick it out longer in England is one of them. At the end of the day it was my choice to return to Scotland with Rangers. I have absolutely no regrets about that or joining Rangers, because they are a great club, but I still wish I had stayed in England for a few more years, just to have been able to learn and develop more as a player. But I was also aware playing for Rangers was a once in a lifetime opportunity and not one I could afford to let pass me by. I knew I was in a privileged position, about to start the next chapter of my career as a Rangers player.

6

HAVE YOU CONSIDERED
ANOTHER CAREER?

WHEN I arrived at Ibrox in 1983 I quickly realised that everything wasn't quite right behind the scenes. It didn't take me long to find out where the problems stemmed from – the dressing room. I could see within days there was a lot of discontent and unhappiness within the squad. A lot of the experienced players, like Derek Johnstone, Colin McAdam and Gregor Stevens, had started to rebel against the manager, John Greig. They were good players and decent guys but they were no longer first-team regulars. John had, for whatever reason, left them out and decided they were no longer central to his or the club's future plans. It certainly didn't help the atmosphere round the place. Crowds at Ibrox weren't great and there wasn't much money about the club, so it was a hard job for Greig and his assistant, Tommy McLean. Their hands were tied because they had to get players out before they could get their own men in. Some of the guys he wanted to move on weren't willing to go and were prepared to sit it out and show their own act of defiance to the manager. It was a Catch-22 situation for all involved and didn't really provide a healthy atmosphere for anyone. I could see both sides. The experienced players had been good and loyal servants to the club and felt they deserved a bit more respect, they also believed they should still have been in the team. I could also understand why John Greig took the stance he did. When I went into management I quickly found out the importance of having your players and dressing room behind you. You are paid to make the big decisions and you have to do what you feel is right for the sake of the team. John decided these players were no longer part of his plans and felt it was in the best interests of the club that he moved them on. I am not saying anybody was right or wrong but the situation certainly didn't help Rangers.

Personally, I was just delighted to be back in Scotland playing for a club with the tradition of Rangers. I was going to give my all, despite what was going on around me, for the club. That, after all, was the reason why I left West Ham. It was a great honour to be playing somewhere like Ibrox every second weekend. I had played there a few times with Airdrie but to run out in the blue and white was something special. I have always been a positive person and I just wanted to do the best I could. You also expect that from the rest of your teammates, although for the reason I stated earlier, it wasn't always the case. It wasn't really a healthy dressing room and it made John Greig's job a lot more difficult than it should have been. Maybe if he had got the players that he wanted out then he could have focused solely on first-team matters but that didn't happen. Instead he had to manage in difficult circumstances, with players who didn't share his vision of how the club should be taken forward.

I just wanted to get my Rangers career up and running. I can still remember my Ibrox debut. It was against Motherwell on 19 March 1983. We won 1–0, with John McClelland scoring the goal. It was good to get off on the right foot, although by that time the league was already out of our grasp, Dundee United, Aberdeen and Celtic were too far ahead. All we could do was salvage some pride, win as many games as we could and try to close the gap. Just days after my debut I made my Old Firm bow at Celtic Park. It was in front of more than 51,000 fans, most of them wearing green and white, so that was an experience in itself. I have played in a lot of derbies but I would say the Old Firm was the most passionate and demanding atmosphere I have ever played in. I just couldn't believe the noise in that game, it was so electric I even struggled to hear my teammates when they were standing next to me. I have been to derbies all over the world and I have never witnessed anything like an Old Firm game. It is a special, special match. In saying that, my first Old Firm game failed to live up to expectations in terms of the football. It ended 0–0 and was far from a classic, although, from our own point of view, it wasn't the worst of results.

I know a lot is made of the religious divide when it comes to Rangers and Celtic but I can honestly hold my hands up and say I have never had any real hassle on that front, outwith one isolated incident when I was away working with the BBC, although I will come to that later. The majority of the Rangers and Celtic support are good people who just want to see their team doing well. You get the occasional nutter but they are few and far between and in difficult situations you know you just have to walk away, but the bulk of Old Firm fans are just passionate supporters who want to talk about the game and their team. I have always enjoyed a pint and I have my local, the Fairway Hotel, in Bathgate. There is a good mix of supporters in there. It is still my local today and I thoroughly enjoy having a pint with the boys in there, I can't write this without mentioning a few of their names. I have to start with the staff. The bar is run by Amnon, who is Israeli by birth and he is aided and abetted by his loyal staff, Stuart, Tam and 'Doobs'. The other side of the bar brings a real mixture of characters, including Colin, Stuart, Shaun, Russell, big Brian, Gareth, Lockie and the two Dereks. They all follow a host of clubs and come from various backgrounds but there is always a great atmosphere in the pub, especially when the big games are on. They all have their opinions and are passionate about their teams but it is all good banter and we all have a good laugh and a joke about things – regardless of results.

My first Rangers goal came against Dundee United at Tannadice but it proved to be anything but memorable as Jim McLean's title chasers thumped us 3–1. We were well beaten. After the game John Greig really had a go at us, you could see he was really stressed and on edge. I remember looking at him and thinking that is not right; you shouldn't be getting yourself in such a state – regardless of your feelings for the club. It was clear that John had piled all the club's problems onto his own shoulders and it was beginning to take its toll on him physically and mentally. He had been used to the very best as a player. He was, quite rightly, voted Rangers' greatest ever player and was desperate to get the team back to those lofty standards. I have seen it plenty of times since with other managers but that was the first time I really saw the pressures of the job. The ironic thing is that was nothing like the real John Greig. He is a jovial character, a winner and loves Rangers but it was just the strain and pressure of managing the expectations of Rangers at that time. I remember I said to myself if I ever go into management then I am never going to let it affect me like that. I don't think I did, although others might tell you differently. What happened to John during that period certainly opened my eyes to management.

My next goal for Rangers was a bit more important. It came when we played St Mirren in the semi-final of the Scottish Cup at Celtic Park. I scored our goal but the Buddies equalised to force a replay at Hampden. I wasn't to be denied my moment of glory. In the second game, I managed to net the only goal of the game in the final minute of extra time. There was a massive dispute as to whether or not the ball had crossed the line. The St Mirren player John McCormack, who I played against many times and is now a good friend, claims to this day that the ball never went in, but I am in absolutely no doubt that it crossed the line. Obviously, that was an important goal because it got us into the cup final, where we would play Sir Alex Ferguson's Aberdeen, who had also done Scotland proud by getting to the final of the European Cup Winners' Cup. For us, the Scottish Cup remained the last chance to land some silverware from what had been another massively disappointing season for everybody at Ibrox. I came into the final in decent form after I had finished the Premier Division campaign with four goals in four games. My final two goals came in our last match of the season, although we lost 4–2 at Ibrox. It was a match we were desperate to win, not only because it was an Old Firm derby but because Celtic were also in with a chance of winning the league, and as a Rangers player that was the last thing we wanted to see. Dundee United and Aberdeen were also in contention. We went 2–0 up and my strikes were somewhat fortuitous; the first was a shot from Davie Cooper that deflected off me and the second was almost a carbon copy, with Davie McKinnon firing a shot off me. In my defence both shots were going well wide; however, Celtic ended up coming back and beat us 4–2. It was a bit of a blow and we were just relieved to hear that Dundee United had beaten Dundee to clinch the title. Our moods would have been ten times worse had Celtic won the league by beating Rangers. We ended up finishing disappointingly in fourth place, eighteen points behind the champions Dundee United, while Aberdeen and Celtic also finished above us. Our form at the end of that campaign was pretty good – we only lost three out of our twelve games before the cup final. The signs were that John Greig was starting to put a decent team together who would finally be capable of challenging for silverware.

We definitely had quality within our ranks. Davie Cooper was the best player I have ever had the good fortune to play with. There was an amazing transformation from 'Coop' to the guy he was when he first started out. I got to know him well because he stayed in Motherwell and I was back in Airdrie. He couldn't drive, and had no intention of driving, so I used to chauffeur him to training and games. He was a great guy but at times he could be an absolute nightmare. He was nicknamed Albert Tatlock after the grumpy character from Coronation Street because of the way he used to take the huff at the slightest thing. There were times in training where he wouldn't talk to any of us. I reckon he could have fallen out with his own shadow, but, to be fair, it never lasted long. If he did take the hump with you he would soon fall back in with you. I remember the day he went in a mood with everybody. We were training and he just took the ball and wouldn't pass to anyone and nobody could get it off him. He kept it to himself for a good few minutes because he was just so skilful and that was with the one foot, the inside and outside of his left peg. He was an incredible talent and when it came to set pieces there were few who were better than 'Coop'. The power he could generate from free kicks was amazing and that was another thing that made him one of the Scottish game's true greats.

Davie was elusive for even the best of defenders but if you were part of the press then you had even less chance of getting him onside. He was pretty quiet and he didn't really want to get involved in that side of the game. I remember we had a press open day at Ibrox before the 1983 Scottish Cup final. We were out training on the pitch and the journalists were told to grab whoever they wanted after we had finished our session. The press were all congregated behind the goal. 'Coop' just kept running to the other end of the pitch whenever anybody came near him, it was funny to watch, if you weren't part of that particular press pack. Knowing the media the way I do now, these guys were only doing their job, and it must have been so frustrating for the guys that day. I think eventually some of the reporters were able to build up a relationship and they got an occasional word from Davie from time to time. Later in his career he did open up a bit more and I think he became an even better person because of that. He was a great player and person and it was just such a sad day when we lost him so early in his life.

We knew if we were to lift the Scottish Cup that 'Coop' would have to be on song. Aberdeen went into the cup final on a high, as they had famously beaten Real Madrid in Gothenburg a few days before. We knew that result would have taken a lot, physically and mentally, out of their players and we were confident that if we could play to our form then we could win the cup. We had also beaten the Dons 2–1 at Ibrox the previous month, so that also gave us a lot of confidence. We certainly gave it a right good go and I don't think anybody could argue that we were the better team over the piece. I remember Billy Davies came on as a substitute for us and hit the bar with a shot that might well have won the game, but then Eric Black managed to nick the only goal of the game for Aberdeen in extra time. It was a real disappointment because we definitely felt we should have won the cup. I think how well we had played and how poor Aberdeen had been was summed up by Sir Alex Ferguson's post-match television interview, where he slaughtered his players just minutes after they had won the Scottish Cup and days after they had lifted the European Cup Winners' Cup. All in all, there had been plenty of pain and very little gain. I had also come off second best in a full-blooded challenge with the Aberdeen goalkeeper Jim Leighton and I ended up hobbling about for weeks after the final. It didn't turn out to be my happiest days. Not that my mood was going to be any brighter with the series of events that were about to follow.

I had started to feel my groin and pelvic area when I was at West Ham. It was nothing serious, just a bit niggly I thought. It certainly didn't stop me playing. The situation had started to get worse in the final weeks of the season. I went down to Largs that summer to start my SFA coaching badges where our assistant manager, Tommy McLean, was taking the course. I told Tommy my groin was causing me a bit of concern and he arranged for me to go and see a specialist at Ross Hall, the private hospital in Glasgow. I went to see him a few weeks later when he did a number of X-rays and also went through a thorough examination of the problem area. He basically told me the right-hand side of my groin area was a complete mess, he showed me the X-ray and it looked moth-eaten, with holes all over it. All he said to me was, 'Have you thought of another career outside of football?' I thought he was having a laugh but he said, 'No, I am being serious. Your groin is really bad and I don't know how an operation will turn out.' I, in a state of total shock, replied, 'But it is only a niggle.' I then thought 'He is the specialist, he must know what he is talking about.' I just walked out of the room completely numb, I was left completely dumbfounded by the bombshell news.

You get a gut feeling about things. I have had them throughout my life and when I finally got my head round things I thought to myself this can't be right. That is a load of rubbish. I had hardly missed a day's training in my life and I was determined I wasn't going to have to hang up my boots. I thought a bit of rest would do it good over the summer, but when I returned to pre-season I was still struggling. I got in touch with my old

Airdrie manager Bobby Watson. He had always sent his Airdrie players up to an orthopaedic surgeon, Mr John Watson, up at Hairmyres Hospital in East Kilbride. Bobby told me to go and speak to John, so I decided to take his advice. I explained the situation and everything that had happened and then he took a look at my groin. He said the best course of action was a cortisone injection so I got the jag. It was horrendously painful but two days later I was flying through pre-season without the slightest bit of bother. That whole affair made me slightly sceptical of specialists who weren't football related. I was just relieved and delighted I was back playing. You didn't hear me grumble through any of that pre-season.

The one thing that did keep me going through that difficult time was the birth of my daughter, Susan, on 23 June 1983. Suzi's arrival helped me take my mind off the football and brought a smile back to my face through a very difficult period.

7

SILVER-LINED WITH SUPER ALLY

I HAD finished the previous campaign playing up front at Rangers with either John MacDonald or Gordon Dalziel. John Greig felt we needed a bit more firepower and went into the market to buy another striker. He ended up going to Sunderland to buy a young Scot by the name of Alastair McCoist, who had moved to Roker Park from St Johnstone. I had played against him a few times when I was at West Ham and also together in that Scottish semi-professional team. Ally had failed to settle to life south of the border. Like me, he had jumped at the chance to return to Scotland when Rangers declared their interest. When I first came across 'Coisty', in that semi-professional tournament in Holland, he made an instant impression on me and it had nothing to do with his football. He had the smelliest feet in the world and was one of the untidiest people I have ever come across.

I felt for Ally because he got a right hard time from the Rangers fans early on. Nothing seemed to come off for him in those early months, but testament to him because he never let his head go down and worked his socks off. Ally was one of the hardest-working professionals in the game. He was good fun to be around, he liked a laugh and a joke, but when it came to the serious stuff he gave absolutely everything. To be fair to Ally, he struggled in a team that was hardly firing on all cylinders. I was a few years older than him and tried to use my own experiences to help him. I had a good few chats and heart-to-hearts with him on how to get back on track and adjust to the pressures of playing for a club the size of Rangers. He might have found it hard but he never wavered, he continued to give his all and eventually got his just rewards when he turned things around. He went on to show what a good footballer and what a great finisher he was.

I went on to room with him at Rangers as I had with the semi-pro side and untidy was an understatement. He certainly hadn't improved his personal hygiene any from that early trip to Holland. He was just a pest, he would go about wearing other people's clothes. We went away round the world with Rangers for a month and he had the smelliest, dirtiest gear. It was sometimes difficult to get things washed but that didn't bother Ally, he would just turn up wearing somebody else's trousers or clothes – it didn't matter who they belonged to. He has such a brass neck you couldn't have marked him with a blowtorch.

That world tour turned out to be a horrendous trip for the team. Bobby Williamson and Colin McAdam broke their legs and Bobby Russell also got badly injured. I was one of the more fortunate ones as I ended up with a head knock that required two or three stitches. That wasn't anything unusual for me, as it happened quite a few times throughout my career. We didn't have a doctor on the trip and the local Australian general practitioner in Adelaide stitched me up before we moved on. Of course, after five days the stitches had to come out and we didn't have anybody to do it, so it was left to 'Doctor McCoist'. Ally pulled them out for me and I don't think my head has been the same since. 'Coisty' is some character – half of the stories you couldn't print but you could bet he would be at the centre of most of the madness. On another trip, he woke up this sleepy Swiss town by rapping in the middle of the main square. He just kept going for hours, entertaining his teammates, the locals and whoever would listen.

Ally went on to have a tremendous career for Rangers and Scotland and is now worshipped by the Rangers support, which is great. He could have quite easily have taken the easy option and walked away when things weren't going for him, but, credit to him, he stuck at it and he has got his just rewards. He went on to be Rangers' record goal-scorer and was a star for club and country. It was also great to see him become Rangers manager after he learned his trade under Walter Smith before getting the chance to manage Rangers in his own right. I know what that meant to him because I saw what Rangers meant to him when he was a player.

Those early weeks of the 1983–84 season were hard for everybody at Rangers. Hope from the previous campaign quickly evaporated when we lost three of our first four league games. We hoped things would click when Ally got a double and I got another as we thrashed St Johnstone 6–3 to register our first league win. We backed that up by beating the champions Dundee United at Tannadice and Hibs at home but then our season completely came off the rails.

We were still in the League Cup and had absolutely annihilated the Maltese minnows Valetta 18–0 on aggregate in the European Cup Winners' Cup, having qualified for the latter competition after losing to Aberdeen in the Scottish Cup final. That saw us paired against the Portuguese giants Porto in the next round. We went 2–0 up after the first leg at Ibrox, I scored the first and Dave Mitchell got our second. We were in a really good position until big Peter McCloy threw one in near the end. Results domestically were still indifferent and John Greig resigned before the second leg in Portugal.

He had decided enough was enough and he wasn't going to turn things around. Greig's record over the piece wasn't the worst and he also made a few signings during his time at the Ibrox helm. Funnily enough, he bought Jimmy Nicholl just before he departed, Jimmy came up the road and signed on the Thursday and John resigned the next day. I always tell Jimmy that John had quickly realised what a mistake he had made!

Rangers were actively searching for a new manager, somebody who could get them back challenging. The New Firm had overtaken the Old Firm and that was down to the management of Jim McLean at Dundee United and Sir Alex Ferguson at Aberdeen. As players, we were always the last to know who was in the frame to become our new manager. There had been a lot of press speculation that Rangers had tried to appoint both Ferguson and McLean, and McLean was also seen coming out of Ibrox. I think they maybe came closer to appointing McLean than Ferguson but in the end neither move came off. The Ibrox board were forced to look further down their A list and because we were midway through our season the board were under pressure to get a manager in. Tommy McLean was put in temporary charge, although his cause wasn't helped when we lost 1–0 away to Porto to go out on away goals.

Jock Wallace was a Rangers legend. He had managed the club previously and had famously guided the team to two glorious trebles. The Ibrox board obviously felt he could help the club recapture some of those former glories. There is no doubt his appointment lifted the entire club. What you saw with Jock was what you got, he was a man's man but he also had this aura about him. You knew there would be something to fear if you stepped out of line. He was in charge and there were no ifs or buts about that. There was none of the rumblings of discontent we had seen in the dressing room under John Greig. Jock was a very, very fair man; if you did something wrong then you paid the price, with a slap on the back of the head or a kick up the backside.

'Coisty' was normally the one who faced his wrath. As everybody knows, timekeeping has never been Ally's strong point. He is always late or gets there just in the nick of time and is never early for anything. Ally is so laid back. He would be sitting there watching the television or biting his nails and then would suddenly run about mad at the last minute to get there. I don't know how many times Big Jock slaughtered him or even fined him for being late. Ally didn't bother. He paid his fine, shrugged things off and went back on his merry way. There was one incident where I was to blame for getting us both a right rollicking. It was when we were flying out on that world tour and we went via Heathrow Airport. Ally and I had jumped off the plane and I told him to follow me because I had almost lived in Heathrow when I had been down at West Ham. So we started walking to the other terminal to catch our connecting flight out to Australia. We eventually got to the gate and there was nobody else there. Unbeknown to us, Big Jock had organised a bus outside the other terminal to transfer all the players. Everybody was sitting on this bus waiting for us. We were getting called all the names under the sun and when the bus finally arrived at the departures lounge Jock came down to the terminal gate and called us for everything. Let's just say he didn't miss us and he left us without a name. It was wee things like that which annoyed Jock because he felt it was a team affair and it was one for all and all for one, it was a lesson we quickly learned.

Big Jock was a passionate, passionate Rangers man. He would fire you up with his tales of war. He would tell us to get the battle fever on and when you put the bayonet in make sure you twist it and kill them off. Basically, telling us to take our chances when they come along. He was also a great man-manager – you knew as your boss he would back you 100 percent, whether you were good or bad!

Jock tried everything he could to get us going. He even changed the home strip back to black socks with red tops but because of our sponsorship deal with Umbro we had to switch back to the red socks until the end of the season. He wanted the pride and passion restored to the club. I remember that first game up in Aberdeen he had us all up the back of the bus singing Rangers songs and getting us to believe in the cause. Everyone was pumped up for the game but we ended up losing an early goal and disappointingly lost 3–0.

Big Jock's personality and his enthusiasm rubbed off on the players and there was an improvement in morale and results as he managed to halt the decline. We put together a fifteen-game unbeaten run in the league and also made the League Cup final. We beat Queen of the South, Clydebank, Hearts and St Mirren along the way before we saw off Dundee United in the semi-final. We drew 1–1 at Tannadice and then goals from Ian Redford and myself at Ibrox set up an Old Firm final.

We were desperate to make up for the disappointment of losing the Scottish Cup final to Aberdeen. We also knew that our poor start to the season had all but ended our championship ambitions so the League Cup was our best hope of a trophy. We were up against Celtic so we knew how important it was to not only win the cup for the club but also for the fans. My initial recollection was that we went into that game a bit short of players. The previous weekend Ian Redford and Robert Prytz picked up suspensions, so our resources were stretched to the limit. I was up front with John MacDonald that day and Ally ended up playing in midfield and a young Dave McPherson also played wide left of the midfield. He was still a teenager and, to be fair to him, he played really well that day, albeit out of position.

It turned out to be some game as 'Coisty' got the hat-trick. It was a great day and a brilliant match, made even better by the fact we got the result, although it was all about 'Coisty'. He got his first goal from the penalty spot. I played a part in his second when I beat big Roy Aitken and pushed the ball on to Ally to score. He got the winner from a second penalty that Pat Bonner saved but he managed to stick away the rebound in extra time.

I still have fond memories from that day. It is the only senior medal I picked up in my playing days. Playing a cup final at Hampden, in an Old Firm game, was a great occasion. It gave me a special feeling, but I don't think it actually sank in for me until later on in my career when I realised it wasn't going to happen again. When you get to that stage then it begins to feel even more special. I would have hated to have gone throughout my entire playing career without having won a major trophy. Winning the League Cup obviously gave everyone at Ibrox hope under Jock Wallace. It also justified my decision to return to Rangers and proved we could win silverware.

I remember when he came back, Big Jock always used the old boot room at Ibrox. He would take out the Subbuteo pitch and players and would use them to set out his tactics. Our next league game was against Celtic. He said, 'You are here and he is there.' He was telling us who was playing and where. He went right through the team but he had named twelve players. We were all sitting there dying to tell him, but we knew he was in full flow and nobody was brave enough to correct him. Then he signed off by saying, 'That's it, come on let's go.' He walked out and we looked at each other and said, 'Well one of us is going to be disappointed.' Eventually we had to go and see his assistant, Alex Totten, to find out the team. I can't remember who ended up missing out but thankfully it wasn't me. I later went into management and I know what an easy mistake Jock had made. I have probably done it myself but it showed his enthusiasm and desire to get us pumped up for the game.

Celtic, however, took their revenge when they beat us at Parkhead 3–0. That was to be the only blip on our Premier Division campaign as we completed the season's run-in unbeaten. The other big disappointment came when we were knocked out of the Scottish Cup after a quarter-final replay defeat at home to Dundee. We signed off with an eight-game unbeaten run in the league but too many draws killed us. We ended up finishing fourth again, with the same three teams above us. This time, Aberdeen were crowned champions and were followed by Celtic and Dundee United. I finished with fourteen goals while Ally finished with twenty-two. There was something to build on.

8

MY IBROX BLUES

THE WRITING looked to be on the wall at Ibrox. Jock Wallace had brought in a few strikers of his own, trying to improve things and get his own team together. One of the players he signed was Bobby Williamson from Clydebank. Bobby had been part-time and working on a building site while playing with the Bankies. So he jumped from there straight into full-time football and it was a bit of a culture shock for him in more ways than one. At that time, I was driving a pretty sporty Opel Manta car. When Bobby first drove up to Ibrox he saw my car, looked at his old banger and then decided to park round the corner so nobody else could see it. Bobby was a good lad who I hit it off with right away and we are still good friends.

Dave Mitchell had also come in from Adelaide City at the end of the previous season although it wasn't until big Jock arrived that he really made an impact at Ibrox. He was born in Glasgow but spent most of his formative years out in Australia. Dave was another good lad, he was limited technically but was always willing and worked really hard to improve his technique and those attributes, to his credit, ended up helping him to carve out a half-decent career for himself, with the likes of Chelsea, Feyenoord, Eintracht Frankfurt and the Australian national team. We also had Ally McCoist and Iain Ferguson, who Jock had signed from Dundee.

I knew I wasn't one of Jock's signings and it also didn't help that I continued to play with a niggling groin problem. I probably needed rest more than anything, but I kept putting myself forward. I was desperate to play and help the team turn the corner. I was taking anti-inflammatory tablets and painkillers just to get through the matches. I knew things weren't right but I refused to give in. My leg would have needed to be hanging off for me not to make myself available, although I admit my form definitely suffered as a result, I never got near the sort of levels I knew I could.

I found myself in and out of the team. I was no longer an automatic first-pick as Jock was trying to work towards the 1984–85 season. He also brought Colin McAdam and Derek Johnstone back into the set-up as well. Both these guys could also play up front if needed so there was a lot of competition. I don't know if Jock was under pressure to cut his wage bill and move people on but I knew my time was up when Jock came to me and asked if I would be interested in going on loan to Hong Kong Rangers. Both clubs had a tie up and quite a few players had made the journey from Ibrox to go out and get games. I am just relieved I didn't make that move because I ended up losing my dad, Rab, that November. That was sore enough but it would have been ten times harder for me if I had been on the other side of the world.

I knew myself I wasn't setting the heather alight so the last thing I needed to hear was one of my teammates having a go at me. It came after I had missed a shot in training. Robert Prytz turned around and laughed and then totally slaughtered me. His words were like a red rag to a bull, I just completely lost it and turned and smashed him in the face. I wish I could say it immediately made me feel better but as soon as I did it I felt absolutely awful. I knew we all needed to be together, fighting

A chip off the old block – my dad, Rab, and me.

A rough diamond.

Mum's the word – my mum, Margaret, and me.

A football education at Caldervale High.

Some managers have told me I have been a bit of a cowboy at times.

My teacher and Airdrie teammate Derek Whiteford shows us how to hit the heights.

I celebrate scoring a goal against Partick Thistle – while Alan Rough looks on in dismay.

Local hero – beating Motherwell's Hugh Sproat to help fire us back into the top flight.

Back in the big-time – the 1979-80 Airdrie team celebrate promotion to the Scottish Premier Division.

A team game – I celebrate my First Division Player of the Year Award with my Airdrie teammates.

Firing Rangers to Hampden – my controversial Scottish Cup semi-final winner versus St Mirren.

Skipping past Celtic's Danny McGrain in the Skol Cup final.

Jumping on Ally McCoist as we celebrate his Skol Cup final winner.

Celebrating our Skol Cup final win with my Rangers teammates.

Alex MacDonald and Sandy Jardine welcome me to Hearts.

Hibs keeper Alan Rough comes out to challenge me in the derby.

Strike partners – celebrating a derby goal with John Robertson

Battling with Dundee's Colin Hendry on that ill-fated day.

Hearts chairman Wallace Mercer tries to console a distraught fan.

Watching Albert Kidd sink our title dream at Dens Park.

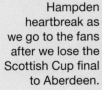

Hampden heartbreak as we go to the fans after we lose the Scottish Cup final to Aberdeen.

Batman and Robin – or John Robertson and me.

Craig Levein, Brian Whittaker and myself get ready to do more derby damage to Hibs.

Trying to keep the peace as tensions threaten to boil over with Rangers player-manager Graeme Souness.

© ERIC MCCOWAT

Me with my Scottish Professional Footballers Association Player of the Year trophy for the 1981-82 season.

© CRAIG HALKETT

on the pitch not on the training ground. Jock Wallace didn't even say anything though. I think he just turned a blind eye to it. He had bigger issues to address than to worry about a minor training ground flare-up.

To be fair to Robert, he apologised right away and admitted he shouldn't have said anything. I also said sorry because I knew I had been wrong and shouldn't have punched him. That was the one good thing to come out of the whole sorry situation; Robert never had a go at me out on the training park again. Robert was one of the few players I had physical contact with. It came at a time when the team and I, in particular, were struggling, nothing seemed to be going our way and it wasn't down to a lack of trying, but we were well short of the likes of Dundee United, Aberdeen and, even worse, Celtic. The fans were, quite rightly, on our backs because a great team like Glasgow Rangers should have been up there challenging with the best.

Robert was a big character in our dressing room. He arrived at Ibrox the previous season from Swedish side Malmo and he was a talented midfielder that was borne out by the fifty-six caps he won for Sweden and the playing career he had, including his famous spell out in Italy with Hellas Verona. But there were times when he was his own worst enemy. He was just too laid back for his own good. He was also the joker in the pack and always had something to say. Jimmy Nicholl wound Robert up silly one night. The boys were all out in Glasgow and this girl came into the bar, with let's just say a slight imperfection. Right away, Robert made a smart comment about her. Jimmy just stared back at him with a face like thunder and then shouted at him, 'Do you know my sister has a similar issue and in my eyes you have just insulted her.' You should have seen Robert's face – it was a picture, he didn't know where to look. He obviously tried to apologise to Jimmy and said he should never have said what he did but Jimmy was having none of it and this went on for hours. Jimmy just kept it going and going. Robert was made to feel worse with every passing second that his teammate gave him the cold shoulder. It got to a point later where Robert almost ended up in tears and Jimmy finally decided to cave in and tell him it had all been a massive wind-up. It certainly sorted Robert out that night but rest assured he was back to his normal, bullish self the next day in training.

I had bigger concerns as I continued to struggle with a bad groin and pelvic injury that definitely hindered my time at Ibrox. I decided to put my faith in the hands of another specialist at Ross Hall Hospital in Glasgow because I just couldn't get to the bottom of the injury. I tried to play through the pain barrier but, in the end, I just couldn't do it because the pain was so bad. I ended up making the injury worse and in the process didn't do myself or the team justice. Thankfully, the injury only needed a bit of rest and time to get me back to full fitness.

Hearts then declared their interest at the start of that 1984–85 season. Alex MacDonald was desperate to take me to Tynecastle, I had made just two starts for Rangers and so I was desperate to hear what he had to say. I went to speak to Alex but right away I thought there was no chance the deal would happen. I was on £300 a week, as all the players were at Rangers, and Hearts couldn't get anywhere near that. They were struggling financially, Wallace Mercer had not long taken over and was trying to guide them through some difficult and trying financial times. Alex and his assistant, Sandy Jardine, were attempting to rebuild Hearts and to get them up to where they should be, at the top end of Scottish football, but Hearts' basic wage was £130 a week. It was an almighty drop and I told them there was no way I could even consider taking such a hit. My situation was also more complicated because I had split from my first wife, Anne. It was all completely amicable, there was no acrimony over the split, we had just drifted apart. If am being honest we probably got married too young but I still kept in touch with Anne and still regularly got to see my daughter, Suzi. I went back to staying with my mum and dad in their council house back in Airdrie.

Alex MacDonald was trying everything in his power but, as a former Rangers player, he knew the financial gulf that existed between the wage structures of both clubs. I was still keen to go, if a deal could be agreed. I wasn't playing every week at Rangers and I had to make a decision: do I go or do I stay and fight and hope I can get back in the team? I spoke to Alex and Wallace Mercer again a couple of weeks later. Wallace came up with one of his scams to try and get my money up, but a lot of it was incentive-based and was dependent on how successful the team was. He gave it the big sales pitch and told me everything I wanted to hear. You knew there was a certain amount of flannel with him but there was also a bit of belief there as well. An entrepreneur was the best way to describe Wallace. He had been a property developer and had quite a few pubs at one point.

I don't know how hopeful Alex MacDonald was of doing a deal because he also declared an interest in another striker, who would later to go on to become a favourite for Hibs and Rangers, in Gordon Durie. He was still a young striker at the time with East Fife and if he hadn't got me then I am pretty certain that Alex would have signed Gordon, although his preference was always to try and add more experience to his squad.

Eventually we managed to get a deal done. Hearts were paying low wages but were offering big bonuses. Wallace said he would give me a £7,000 signing-on fee but over the course of the three years that were left on my Rangers contract. It still meant I would have been taking a massive cut, one I couldn't afford to take. Eventually I said the bonuses are great and I hope we do win but if you want me to come then you have to make up any shortfall come the end of the season. Basically if we had done well then I would have been better off and if we struggled then Wallace would guarantee my wage to take me back up to my £15,000 a year. The incentive was there to do well, which was the right way to go about things. Wallace accepted my proposal and the two clubs agreed a fee for my services. Alex just wanted the deal to happen and was delighted to get me. It only cost Hearts £35,000 and they were that hard up they had to make fourteen payments of just over £2,500 a month. That showed what a bad state Hearts were in, they were skint.

It was time to pack the bags and make the trip along the M8. My time with Rangers wasn't the greatest spell of my career and it definitely wasn't the most successful spell in Rangers' history either but it was still great to play there. It was a difficult time for everyone at Ibrox. Remember that was the period before the money was really pumped into the club, just before the Graeme Souness revolution. I still loved playing there and I had a good partnership with Ally McCoist. They might have been difficult times for the club but there were also some happy times as well. Rangers are a great football club with a great tradition and they had some great people working at the club. John Greig signed me as manager and I still talk to him when I see him. The late Jock Wallace went on to replace him as manager and he also offered me a lot of advice as a player and as a person. He was the manager who sold me but I have nothing but good things to say about Big Jock. I was at his funeral in Edinburgh and that was a sad day. There was a massive turnout and that, for me, just shows what a great man and legend of Scottish football he was. It was great to play for Rangers, I loved every minute of it. My only regret was that for a lot of my time there the Rangers fans just didn't see the best of me.

9

A HEARTFELT MOVE

I QUICKLY realised how bad things were financially at Hearts the day I was unveiled at Tynecastle. John Binnie was a coach at the club and went on to become No. 2 to Alex MacDonald when they moved on to Airdrie. John told me that whenever Wallace signed a player he held a big do with all the press up in the boardroom. To be fair to Wallace, he was always good value and collected quite a few headlines throughout his time at Hearts. The press all loved him because he was such good copy. It was a similar set-up when he unveiled me as a Hearts player. He was sitting there and said something along the lines of, 'Sandy Clark is a wonderful player and the manager and I are delighted to have him.' I was just looking about when I saw a man in a suit walking around the room, picking up things and looking completely oblivious to what else was going on. I asked about him but nobody knew who he was until I later found out that he had been a debt collector. He was putting a value on everything in the boardroom. I was later told he had been in because the club was possibly looking at closure over an unpaid debt and he was looking to claw back some of the money his client was due. Wallace was probably the only other man in the room who knew what had been going on but it didn't bother him in the slightest. He just got on with things as if he didn't have a care in the world. But, to be fair to Wallace, he always dealt with things and would scrape through, one way or another.

My initial thoughts were, what have I done? I was eventually assured that Hearts would survive and was able to get on with the job in hand of trying to win over the Hearts support. I made my debut against Morton in the October and scored the winner which made it a good start. My spell of inactivity at Rangers also ended up working in my favour. It allowed my injury to clear up and that was the one silver lining of the whole thing. I was just desperate to play and things worked out well for me under Alex MacDonald.

We went on a decent unbeaten run. Another highlight was my two-goal haul in our 3–2 win over St Mirren on 10 November 1984. It was a day that started well but turned into a day of personal heartbreak and loss. My dad had said to me that morning that he had been feeling a bit fluey and wasn't going to come to the game, he was going to stay in the house and listen to the football on the radio. I didn't think too much of it. After the game at Paisley I headed back into Glasgow to have a night out with some of my old Rangers teammates. I had a few beers and I was just about to head into the city centre when I decided to phone home to check everything was okay. I made the call and my sister-in-law, Helen, answered and told me my dad had passed away, one of the arteries to his heart had ruptured. I stood there in a state of shock. I had probably had too much to drink but I immediately jumped into the car and drove home to Airdrie as quickly as I could. He was only fifty-six and it came as a total shock to everyone. It was a real blow for me and the rest of the family. My dad had been an inspiration to us all and somebody we all looked up to. The only positive, for me, was the fact I had moved back in with my mum and dad after my marriage had broken up. This is something I am thankful for because it allowed me to spend a lot more time with my dad in his final few months, especially those Sunday afternoons together in the Clarkston Miners Welfare Club.

I was lucky because football also gave me a release and something to focus on through what was a very difficult time for the entire family. Being in a dressing room environment can often be the best way to lift your spirits. We had a good squad of players at Tynecastle; we probably could be placed into two groups, the older and younger lads. I was obviously amongst the older boys with Roddy MacDonald, Brian Whittaker, Walter Kidd and Henry Smith. In my first season we also had guys like Donald Park, Willie Johnston and Jimmy Bone. Then there was the younger generation, like Gary Mackay, John Robertson, Craig Levein and Kenny Black. We might have socialised in a couple of groups but we were still very much a team on the pitch. The Christmas party used to be a big night in the social calendar. There were times when all the players would hit the town in fancy dress. There was one year when we decided to put all these daft costumes in a hat and then had to pick out what we would be wearing. It was quite funny because I drew out Robin and my strike partner, John Robertson, picked out Batman. We thought that it would probably be better, as I was bigger, if I went as the caped crusader and he tagged along as my sidekick.

We all got on well and there was always a lot of banter and pranks going on in and round the dressing room. The thing about Hearts was that we didn't have the best of gear but we made the best of what we had. You knew if you were last in you were lucky to get a pair of socks. We would then go training on public parks at Roseburn or at Stenhouse and most of the time we had to either clear up the mess left by dogs or play round it. We certainly weren't pampered like some of the players are today but we used that to our advantage. It became a strength and a motivation that brought us closer together – to go out and get success on the pitch.

I used to travel in from the Glasgow side with Roddy MacDonald, Stuart MacLaren and Brian Whittaker. We were later joined by Iain Jardine when he arrived the following season and we used to meet up at Newhouse and drive together up the M8 to Edinburgh. We would take turns although it was always a challenge trying to get Roddy to drive. He was tighter than two coats of paint and would avoid spending money whenever he could.

There was a fish merchant, Davie Speed, who was a big Hearts supporter. Every week he would come to the club and give you as much fish as you wanted in exchange for a couple of match tickets. Roddy would take that much fish that we thought he had opened a chip shop. All the boys joked that Roddy was so tight that he made his family eat fish on Christmas Day.

One day the M8 brigade decided to put Roddy's love of fish to the test. Brian Whittaker got some fish and stuck it behind one of the panels in Roddy's car and turned up the heating. Suddenly every one of us was absolutely delighted to take their share of the driving, just to avoid sitting in Roddy's car. With every passing week the stink and stench would get worse and worse. Roddy had no idea where it was coming from. He ended up taking his car to a garage where they eventually stripped it down and removed the offending fish, I would have hated to see what sort of state it was in when they took it out. It still took another few weeks before Roddy got the smell out of his car. I still don't know, to this day, if Roddy is aware that it was

Brian Whittaker and the rest of his travelling crew who were the men responsible for this fishy tale.

It certainly put fish off the menu for a while after that, although it was never going to kill the appetite of the M8 brigade. We used to rush away after training every day and head for the local burger van to stock up on sausage and bacon rolls and hamburgers for the journey back. It doesn't fit into the modern day diets of today's footballer but it didn't do us any harm.

Wallace Mercer took a bit of a financial gamble when he signed me. The good thing is that the team did quite well finishing seventh and so the bonuses we pocketed that season meant he didn't have to make up any shortfall in my loss of earnings. Financially, I actually ended up being a bit better off than if I had stayed at Rangers. I think I ended up pocketing £22,000 which was a fair bit more than what my basic wage had been at Ibrox, considering I hadn't been at Tynecastle all season.

I finished the 1984–85 season as our second top scorer with twelve goals, behind John Robertson. 'Wee Robbo' came out top of the scoring charts but I always joked that I set up the majority of them. There were some real highlights for me including my goals in the derby. It was always special to score for Hearts against the Hibees. There was silverware too, although not the one I was looking for, when we won the Tennent's Sixes at Ingliston. We beat Morton 4–1 in the final and I was part of the squad although I would never say six-a-side was my forte. I only ended up playing because so many of the other boys didn't want to.

The team were still establishing themselves in the top flight and seventh spot was a decent showing. It was fairly early in Alex MacDonald's charge, he was still trying to get his squad together and it was a bit of a transitional period for Hearts as some of the older players, like Jimmy Bone and Willie Johnston, started to come to the end of the road. The good thing was that we still had plenty of young talent for the future.

10

THE DAMNED DOUBLE

WE KNEW there were genuine signs of progress at Hearts but even I was surprised at just how much we kicked on in the 1985–86 season. It started when Alex MacDonald decided to break from tradition and take us away to Germany for pre-season. That was a good trip for building up the confidence and self-belief ahead of the new campaign. We opened up in the league by drawing 1–1 with Celtic at Tynecastle. It proved to be the perfect introduction for our new signing, John Colquhoun, who scored our goal against the club he had just left. We hoped that result would be a statement of intent but it wasn't the case. We got thumped 6–2 at St Mirren and lost 3–1 at Rangers – as I got myself sent off, but I will go into that later. The only result we picked up was a 2–1 win over Hibs – in the derby – which went some way to keeping the Hearts fans on side.

We slipped up at Clydebank in a game where Alex MacDonald came off the bench to make his final senior performance. He decided it was time to hang up the boots and concentrate on the management front. It was probably a good decision for the team although nobody could ever knock the quality Alex offered as a player. I played with and against him and to say he is one of the top players that Scotland has produced is an understatement. He was ferocious, not the biggest but he had a magnificent left foot, was decent on his right and excellent in the air. He could also look after himself. If you kicked him in a game you knew you were going to get it back because he wouldn't stop until he had taken his revenge. Those impressive attributes stood him in good stead for management because he was a real winner. Therefore, Alex was as frustrated as anyone with the way results had gone through that period.

It wasn't until the October when we drew with Dundee that things finally clicked into place and that was the start of an amazing unbeaten run. We then went out and beat Celtic 1–0, Walter Kidd swung a ball into the back post, where I was able to bully Danny McGrain and cushion a header down for John Robertson to score the only goal. That was another example of me taking all the knocks and 'Wee Robbo' grabbing the glory. To be fair to John, he was also responsible for getting the team quite a few win bonuses throughout the years with his goals from nothing. We then beat champions Aberdeen thanks to a Craig Levein goal and on the back of those two wins people started to sit up and take notice of Hearts.

Confidence was sky-high and we just kept going. I got in on the act when I scored twice as we thumped Rangers 3–0, though one of my strikes was rather bizarre because I scored with my sock, after I had lost my boot in the build-up. That shows how much the game has changed because you would never be allowed to play on if that was to happen today. Those goals were in the middle of a decent run for me personally. I scored a couple against Motherwell and another in our thrashing of Clydebank, which helped push us up to second spot in the league. Things snowballed with every result. We had a core of a team and it was pretty much the same players week in week out. We were confident and believed we could get a result against anyone.

We gave our fans the ideal Christmas present when we beat St Mirren, courtesy of a penalty from Kenny Black, to go top of the table. It was good to beat the Buddies after they had embarrassed us earlier in the campaign. Looking back, it was actually in rather bizarre circumstances that we went top. Scotland were involved in a World Cup qualifying campaign and ended up in a two-legged play-off against Australia. We hardly had any internationalists in our squad and so we were able to go out and play the majority of our games but the likes of Dundee United, Celtic, Rangers and Aberdeen all had matches cancelled and postponed because of international commitments. That allowed us to get up a head of steam on the others. We put points on the board and put the pressure on our rivals to go out and win their games in hand.

I have to laugh because we had a really good season but it certainly flew in the face of the modern game, where there is so much emphasis put on sports science. Alex MacDonald just kept things simple. If we won on a Saturday then we would be off on a Sunday and Monday, we would come in for a double session of football and fitness on a Tuesday and then we would get a Wednesday off. We would then come back in for a morning session on the Thursday and a half-hour loosener on the Friday and that was it. All in all, some weeks we were lucky to do six hours of training. We enjoyed our nights out and daily trips to the burger van, but when it was time to work on the training pitch and in the matches we always gave our all. We just enjoyed our football and never spoke about winning the league because we were as surprised as anyone how things panned out that year. We couldn't wait for each game to come and we never looked too far ahead. Alex MacDonald and Sandy Jardine were good at keeping our feet on the ground, along with our coaches Walter Borthwick and John Binnie. We were also lucky we were such a closely-knit group, we didn't have any big superstars. John Robertson scored a lot of the goals but he was still relatively young. He was probably our star player but there were no huge egos or big-time Charlies in our dressing room. We were a team and that was our strength.

We just kept going and never got carried away – although there was one afternoon where I ended up on a stretcher. It came when we played Rangers in the Scottish Cup at Tynecastle. The game would never have been played today because the pitch was rock-hard and we had to wear Astroturf trainers. I went up for a challenge with my former Rangers teammate, Craig Paterson. He headed the ball away and then we clashed heads. We have both discussed that incident many times since and neither of us have a clue what actually happened. We were told the blood was gushing out of both our heads and I was knocked unconscious for a second or so. I was carted off but tried to get back on, although the cut was, obviously, a bit bigger than I had realised and the physio, Alan Rae, refused to let me return. Craig also went to the hospital to get stitches inserted in his wound and Doctor Melville, despite having the shakiest hands I have ever seen, attended to my head and stitched me back up. I still have the scar, along with a good few others that I have collected throughout my career. The Doc stitched me up umpteen times throughout my time at Tynecastle. I was told that I couldn't play in the next game against Clydebank, but I decided to ignore medical advice and make myself available and managed to score four minutes from time to rescue us a point.

We continued to put wins on the board although we drew at home to Aberdeen. I remember Wallace Mercer being really annoyed before the match because the league had agreed to switch the game to the Sunday to accommodate television. It was the first time that season we didn't play our weekend fixture on a Saturday. Nobody at Hearts wanted to change our routine but we had to bow to the television company who was putting their money on the table. Peter Weir scored to put Aberdeen ahead before John Colquhoun levelled to give us a point. We didn't lose but I genuinely believe moving that game knocked us out of sync and proved costly.

We were still in the driving seat going into the final two games and Gary Mackay settled the nerves with the only goal at Clydebank. We had one final game at Dens Park against Dundee and we knew if we avoided defeat there then we would be champions. Celtic still had a game in hand against Motherwell and then they were to play St Mirren on the final day. They had to win both their games, get a massive swing in the goal difference and hope that European-chasing Dundee beat us. The odds were firmly stacked in our favour.

Celtic played Motherwell in a midweek fixture. My wife, Liz, and I were staying in a flat at the Furlongs in Hamilton and we could actually see the Fir Park floodlights out of our window. We knew it could be a massively important game for us, but I tried desperately to avoid the result. We were hoping for a Motherwell win and, in the end, curiosity got the better of me. I turned to the radio to find out what was happening, but the news wasn't good as Celtic got the win they needed.

The good thing was that the league still remained in our hands. If we won it didn't matter what happened to Celtic in Paisley. The build-up to the final game against Dundee set the alarm bells ringing. A flu bug hit Tynecastle and floored quite a few of our squad. It definitely upset our preparations because up to that point our team had a pretty settled look about it. Roddy MacDonald managed to shrug off the bug to play, as did Brian Whittaker, although Craig Levein had to call off. Craig was a magnificent player for us and was a big loss. That day he was replaced by Roddy MacDonald and, to be fair to him, I thought he was our man of the match at Dens Park. Iain Jardine and Kenny Black had also been struggling with injuries.

I went into that last game with exactly the same feeling as I had all the way through our run. I just wanted to get out there and play. The incentive was there for us to go and make history and win the league. It was massive but it didn't feel any different to any other game. I just wanted to go out and win. As professionals we just had to go out and do our jobs as best we could.

It was also a massive game for Dundee. Everybody seemed to forget that and dismissed them, even though they still had a chance of qualifying for the UEFA Cup. Granted, that wasn't a bigger carrot than the one we had dangling in front of us.

I got a feeling it wasn't going to be our day. It all stemmed from the infamous penalty that never was, after Colin Hendry brought me down. It came from a throw-in down our left, I turned Colin on the goal line and he stuck his thigh out and knocked me over. It was a stonewall penalty. Bill Crombie was the referee and if he had done his job right that day and given the correct decision then I believe Hearts would have won the league. What I would state on the record was that Bill was a top referee. I had a lot of respect for him, he had handled a lot of Hearts games and I had always got on well with him. I just felt he was put in an impossible position when he was asked to referee that match. I have met Bill on several occasions since but I have never been able to ask him why he never gave us that penalty. It still hurts so much. I don't really need to ask him because I know it should have been a penalty. It was such a momentous decision and one that I, Bill and every Hearts fan will have to live with for the rest of our lives.

I believe the football authorities made an absolute mess of things by appointing Bill to our game. Everyone knew Bill was a Hearts fan, it put enormous pressure on him and it was unnecessary. I can't speak for Bill but it certainly looked like he was uncomfortable refereeing that Dens Park clash. The last thing he would have wanted was to be accused of was favouritism towards Hearts but in that penalty call he went too far the other way. It was a blow not to get that decision but the title was still in our grasp, but Dundee, to their credit, played well. We had one or two half-chances but didn't play anywhere near as well as we had in the run-in. We were aware Celtic were turning the screw at Love Street, but the ball still remained in our court. We knew it was up to us to avoid defeat and clinch the championship.

Things then fell apart when Dundee sent on Albert Kidd as a second-half substitute. He put Dundee ahead with seven minutes to go and three minutes later netted a second, which killed off our title dream, as Celtic beat St Mirren 5–0 to win the championship on goal difference.

It was horrendous. That final whistle left me with a real numb feeling and it took me a long time to get over it. Often after a bad defeat you have arguments and fights but that entire Hearts team just sat in the away dressing room of Dens Park in total silence, trying to come to terms with our loss. We were so low and all sat with our heads down or in our hands. I know there were a lot of tears shed by the fans and it was exactly the same in our dressing room. I was absolutely devastated but I tried to remain positive. I clung on to the hope that we could lift the Scottish Cup the following weekend. That gave me a wee bit of hope at the end of a very long and dark tunnel. I wasn't in tears that day, although I certainly felt like crying. As I said, the only reason I wasn't in tears was that my focus had turned to the cup final.

Alex MacDonald actually went into the shower area for a long time and just stood there alone, trying to gather his thoughts. It must have been a real hammer blow to him. He, like the rest of us, had been left devastated by what had happened. He, obviously, had to get himself together before he could say anything and attempt to lift us up again. Alex, to be fair, couldn't say much that could have raised the spirits. The only positive was we still had a visit to Hampden to take on Aberdeen the following weekend. Alex just told us to hang in there and said he couldn't have asked for any more from us because we had put in such a magnificent effort over the course of the season.

I didn't look at the goals from the Celtic game for a long time after. It was painful, too painful. I have since seen the highlights from that game and let me just say it is my belief, and I know a lot of my Hearts teammates and also our fans felt the same way, that the collective team effort from the St Mirren team could have been a lot better. I am friends with one of the players who played for St Mirren that day. I have spoken to him about what happened in that game on several occasions. I know he gave it his all but he has admitted to me that some of his teammates hadn't been so professional that day. Some of them were happy to see Celtic win the league. I am not saying anyone went out to throw the game but when news filtered through that Dundee were winning I think there was less and less resistance in certain areas of the pitch. I suppose the St Mirren players are the only ones who can really tell us what went on at Love Street that afternoon. I know comparisons were made with Dunfermline, when they lost heavily on the final game of the 2002–03 season to eventual champions Rangers. The Celtic star Chris Sutton was critical of Dunfermline's players, but I will address that a little later. I certainly don't think these two matches can be compared.

I know it will sound like sour grapes, but that is the way I feel, although I accept you can't take anything away from what was a very good Celtic team. They had some brilliant players, in Danny McGrain, Brian McClair and Mo Johnston, even though we had a good record against them over the course of that season. We pushed them all the way and, in the end, it just wasn't to be.

I'm not a very superstitious person and that defeat at Dundee will go a long way to explaining why. You can get into daft wee routines when things are going well. Gary Mackay liked to be the last man out of the changing room and a few of the guys had other things they liked to do. I, for some reason, used to wear the same white shirt until we lost a game. Needless to say that season we went on such a good run that my white shirt almost turned grey. My wife, Liz, would tell me to put it in the bin, but I had no intention of changing it no matter how scruffy it looked. After we lost at Dundee the shirt was the first thing that went into the bucket. I have never done anything else superstitious since and had a brand new white shirt for the cup final.

We beat Rangers, Dundee United, St Mirren and Hamilton on the way to Hampden. We were facing a very good Aberdeen team but I honestly believed we could get over the devastation of what had happened in Dundee by beating Aberdeen. There was no point in thinking any other way or there would have been no point in turning up. I felt fine going into the game although I think some of the younger players might have found it a little more difficult, I was certainly up for the challenge. I had never won the Scottish Cup and I was desperate to get my hands on it. We had shown over the course of the season we could beat the best, including Sir Alex Ferguson's side. I knew they would also have fancied their chances because they had winners in their dressing room. I am also certain they would have believed what had happened to us at Dens Park made us even more vulnerable.

We made a decent start. John Robertson had a very good chance at 0–0 but put it over the bar. Normally, the wee man would have stuck it away. When Aberdeen went ahead through John Hewitt I could sense everything draining out of us. After that, Aberdeen went on and quite comfortably won the game 3–0. We also had Walter Kidd sent off – that is another story, which I will go into a little later!

I felt bad after what happened at Dens Park but when the final whistle went at Hampden I have to confess I felt far worse. I can only describe the feeling as an absolute nightmare. It was horrible. It was the worst I have ever felt in my professional career. The tears certainly flowed at the national stadium, it left me with a real numbness and emptiness. It was almost like the feeling you have when you lose somebody close to you. It was awful because I have no doubt we deserved to win something that season, we didn't and that was so hard to take.

I actually learned a real lesson on the way back from Hampden. I was sitting next to Walter Kidd on the coach and he wasn't too bad after everything that had happened, but that was just the way he was. It must have been horrible for him, getting sent off and watching everything slip away. I was just sitting there but I was getting really, really angry and annoyed with Brian Whittaker. He was a good friend of mine, God bless his soul. Brian was sitting there laughing and joking and it really got to me. I was almost in tears with anger at Brian acting the way he did. I just couldn't understand how he could behave like that after everything that had happened. I remember Walter told me to settle down, it is only when you get older and wiser you realise that people deal with adversity in their own way. Brian was always laughing and joking and that was just his way of dealing with the situation, I know now that Brian felt just as bad as me that night.

I could hardly crack a smile and at times I felt like I needed to call the Samaritans. It took us all a long time to get over that season and the Hearts fans certainly played their part in trying to ease our pain. There must have been thousands of them waiting for us when we got back to the Caledonian Hotel in Edinburgh. It was an amazing scene – it was almost as if we had won the cup. They turned out to show their appreciation for what their team had done and that meant a lot to me and all the boys.

I look back now on the 1985–86 season and maybe we had reached the top of the hill and couldn't go any higher, I just don't know. Basically over those last two games we had gone, physically and mentally we had nothing more to give. We had hit the wall. We had a small squad and had achieved an enormous amount of success and maybe the last two games were just a bridge too far. People can say we bottled it but I would deny that was the case. Yes, we ended up empty-handed but I still believe what we did that season was still a great achievement. If we had been a team of bottlers then we would never have been able to put ourselves in a position to win a double in the first place. Now, with the aid of hindsight, I am also in no doubt that Alex and Sandy got our team to overachieve that season. We had punched above our weight.

The good thing was that Alex MacDonald had laid the foundations of a decent Hearts team and to this day they have remained a major force in Scottish football.

11

SCRAPPING WITH MᶜCOIST AND OTHER TYNECASTLE TALES

AT THE start of the 1985–86 season we lost to Rangers at Ibrox. It is a game that I will always remember, for all the wrong reasons. We not only got beat but I also got sent off, along with my Hearts teammate Walter Kidd. I have to say that initially, in my defence, I was trying to keep the peace but that was quickly shattered by a certain Ally McCoist.

Walter Kidd was a real 100 percent player. You could never come across a more honest professional than Walter. During that ill-fated match he broke up the field from right back and the Rangers midfielder Dougie Bell tried to track back with him. Dougie stuck out an elbow and caught Walter in the face. The referee, Dougie Hope, didn't see the incident and Walter reacted furiously and turned and punched Dougie. That sparked a fracas and suddenly Ally, who had been at the other side of the park, started running like a madman towards the mayhem. I was relatively calm but I could see Ally was about to get himself into trouble. I am a good friend of Ally's and so I tried to keep him away from things, but as soon as I looked at Ally I saw he had that psychotic glaze I had seen quite a few times during our playing days together at Ibrox. He was completely out of it, had just lost the plot. I tried to get him out of the way but he turned round and punched me. Ally says he didn't even know it was me. I was a boy from Airdrie and I was taught if somebody hits you then you hit them back even harder. I punched Ally back and that sparked another melee.

We had a young team and at one point Walter Kidd and I were scrapping amongst nine Rangers players. I think we got to the stage where we were ready to take them all on. Peace was eventually restored and then the referee sent off Walter, Ally and myself. I knew I could have few complaints. Dougie Bell, however, managed to get away scot-free and good luck to him because my motto on the field was that you are only guilty if you get caught.

We trooped off and Walter and I were in the shower in the away dressing room when the door opened and in walked the bold Mr McCoist, with a towel round his waist. He said, 'Sandy, I am really sorry, I can't believe I did that to you.' My response was hardly welcoming. I said, 'Why don't you get to f*** before you get it again.' I was still absolutely beaming because I didn't get sent off that often in my career. To be fair, I went back to the Bellahouston Hotel with some of the Rangers players after the game and by then everything had been forgotten. Ally and I were back to being best mates again, although he was slightly happier than me because at least he had a win bonus to buy the beers.

That sorry episode wasn't to end there. Walter, Ally and myself were also hit with a further three-game ban from the Scottish Football Association for our misdemeanours. Ally accepted his punishment but Walter and I, in our wisdom, decided to appeal through the law courts. Hearts fan Ian Corbett, a prominent Edinburgh lawyer, who I would end up using quite a bit over my career, fought our case. In the end, we were told that we wouldn't win because football was self-governing and we would simply be wasting our time and money. We had to accept the ban and just get on with things – so much for trying to keep the peace!

Mr McCoist isn't the only big-name Scottish player I have had on-the-field issues with. I was also left furious by the antics of the Aberdeen captain Willie Miller in the 1986 Scottish Cup final. It still really angers me to this day, the part Miller played in getting Walter Kidd sent off. Aberdeen had already won the game and there was absolutely no need for it. It was all over nothing.

Gary Mackay was deemed to have fouled Frank McDougall and Walter took exception and threw the ball at the Aberdeen striker. Ok, Walter should have known better. He had already been booked but you could understand his frustrations, with the way the previous week had gone and the fact he knew our double dream was in tatters. Aberdeen were 3–0 up, they already had one hand on the cup, but Willie still felt the need to run thirty to forty yards to get to the referee, Hugh Alexander, so he could shout and scream at him to get Walter sent off. That disgusted me; it really, really annoyed the life out of me and it still does.

Willie's view will have been that he was only doing the best for Aberdeen and was only applying some pressure on the referee to get Walter sent off. I hate it when players try to get fellow professionals sent off. It is one of the things in football that really annoys me. In my view, Willie should have kept right out of things rather than trying to influence the referee. It was something that infuriated me and I didn't forget it in a hurry. The following season I made the Scotland defender more than aware of my feelings. Whenever I got the chance I stuck the boot into Willie for what he did to Walter that day at Hampden. There was one point where Alex McLeish, his central defensive partner for club and country, asked, 'Why do you have it in for Willie?' All I said to Alex was, 'Willie knows fine what he has done.'

There are also countless stories from my time in the Tynecastle dressing room, but unfortunately there aren't that many I would be allowed to put into print. I came across so many great players, characters and people but there were none bigger than the chairman Wallace Mercer. He was a shrewd and successful businessman but I still laugh every time I think back to his signing negotiations with Iain Ferguson. Wallace pulled off some great deals during his time in charge of Hearts but even he would have admitted that signing Iain from Dundee United in 1988 was not one of his best. It had nothing to do with Iain's abilities. He was a top striker and somebody I had played with at Rangers, but there was no doubt Wallace ended up doing himself and the club in financially during those negotiations.

Iain tells the story and it is still hilarious to this day. His agent was Bill McMurdo. Bill had done a few deals with Wallace and also had John Robertson on his books. Bill had a good relationship with Wallace – but that didn't help him in this particular deal. Wallace was desperate to get the transfer pushed through, he told 'Fergie' what his basic wage was and he would get a signing-on fee of £10,000. Wallace phoned Bill and left a message telling him he wanted the deal done and the signing-on fee would be £10,000. Wallace didn't realise that Bill had gone off on holiday and didn't pick up his message. The next day Wallace called Bill again and left another message, along the lines of, 'I need this deal done. You can have the same basic package and a final offer of £15,000 as a signing-on fee but I want it signed today.' Bill was still on holiday. The following day Wallace phoned Bill again and left a third message. This time the signing-on fee was up to £20,000. Bill came back home later that day. He didn't crack a light that he had been away and phoned Wallace right away to agree the deal and accept the £20,000 for his client. Wallace is the only chairman I know that has lost £10,000 to an answer machine.

Another wee story that makes me laugh is when I think back to the antics of the late Brian Whittaker. Some of our car journeys along the M8, from Newhouse to Edinburgh, were chaotic, to say the least, and normally involved Roddy MacDonald, Iain Jardine and Brian. It was an experience when you got into one of Brian's cars, he always bought the cheapest pile of junk he could find. There was a spell when he was driving this old green Morris, which I don't think had any tax or insurance. This car was in such a state of disrepair that he would have been lucky to get either. I remember we were late for training and we were coming down the road in this old banger at Stenhouse in Edinburgh. Brian went up the outside lane and tried to cut in. The next thing we knew he had his credit card up at the window pretending he was an undercover policeman to the car in the inside lane. Unknown to Brian he was trying it on with a real detective and was greeted with a genuine warrant card. The next thing we knew we had been pulled over and Brian was standing there on the pavement, getting a flea in his ear and being told not to be so stupid in future. We were sitting in the car in hysterics, we could see Brian was in a real panic, especially as he had no tax or insurance. He got the fear of his life. I think he thought he would be heading for the nearest police station but he got away with a warning and was sent packing. It was just as well the policeman never looked at Brian's tax disc or asked for his insurance documents because he really would have been in trouble.

When you are a footballer you are quite often asked to do some mad things, like posing on a horse or a motorbike. You are also asked to do a lot of promotional and sponsorship work from time to time. I remember we were asked to record the Hearts Song as a seven-inch single. We did it in a basement studio in Glasgow and it was the funniest thing ever, although probably not to anyone who has had the misfortunate to listen to it. That version was sponsored by Marshall's Chunky Chicken and so it started and finished with their wee advertising jingle. That was bad enough but the singing in between was even worse. At least the jingles were in tune. I don't think there was one player from that Hearts squad of the mid-80s who could hold a note. It was even worse because we had to stand there and sing wearing bright yellow jerseys with a chicken on the front. Let us just say it didn't trouble the charts and I don't know if it did too much for Marshall's Chunky Chicken sales either – outside of Gorgie. I still have a dusty version of the record up in the loft but it has yet to make it on to iTunes.

12

KINGS OF THE CAPITAL

YOU ALWAYS get teams throughout your career that you love playing against and you know you are going to have a good game against. I don't know what it was about Hibs but things just clicked for me and for everybody else connected with Hearts when it came to the derby. Gary Mackay and John Robertson can also point to impressive personal records against the Hibees. We were lucky enough to have played in a Hearts team that had such a good record when it came to capital clashes. I felt going into every game we would beat Hibs or at the very worst have to settle for a draw. We had a great belief, and it didn't matter if the game was at Tynecastle or Easter Road. It was actually probably easier when we went to Leith because there was always so much pressure on Hibs to try and end our run. I always loved playing at Easter Road because it was a decent old stadium and was a good hunting ground for Hearts.

I also used to take so much stick off the Hibs fans. If I had a pound for every bit of abuse I took off them then I would be sitting here as a multi-millionaire, I took absolute pelters. I always wore my heart on my sleeve and gave everything for Hearts. The more stick that came my way the more it would fire me up. I never got involved with the fans, even though there were times when the abuse did become pretty personal and over the top, especially when we were beating them. I always took their stick as a compliment because it meant I must have done something right against their team. Also, the more abuse you got from the Hibs fans the more the Hearts supporters got behind you. It was a win-win situation.

The Hibs manager Alex Miller must have been absolutely demented. He tried everything he could to change their fortunes, like playing in their away strip, mixing up his tactics, players and even his preparations, but nothing seemed to work for him. We knew we had better players and a better team and, inevitably, we went out and showed that. Further down the line I did feel a certain amount of sympathy for Miller because his predicament became a standing joke in our dressing room. We would all laugh and take bets on what Alex would try and change going into the next derby. We used to joke that he would need to change his whole team but that was never going to happen!

Personally, I knew that whatever Hibs defender I was up against I could get the better of them, whether it be Neil Cooper, Tommy McIntyre, Gordon Hunter, Dave Beaumont, Gordon Rae or Ally Brazil. It didn't matter who I was playing against because I knew if I got the right service then I could help supply John Robertson and John Colquhoun round about me. Don't get me wrong, Hibs had some decent players coming through in the later years, like John Collins and Paul Kane, but they never had enough collectively, as a team, to cause us too many problems.

A lot of our belief came from our management team of Alex MacDonald and Sandy Jardine. Alex knew how to work the press and the situation. When it came to the games he got into our heads and made sure that when we walked onto the pitch we would give it our all. I think that can be said about every derby game we played under Alex and Sandy, they would never let us take anything for granted. Alex would always tell us the only reason we had been so successful in this fixture was because of hard work, wanting to win more than them and showing the right qualities at the right time on the pitch. Also, when that first whistle goes in a derby you know the fans would never let you become complacent.

Gary Mackay is as big a Hearts fan as there is and he used to love beating Hibs more than anybody I have come across. He put an incredible amount of passion into those games. You had to settle him down before kick-off because he wouldn't sit in peace. He would be hyper and run around geeing up the rest of the lads. He probably lost a lot of his energy before a ball was kicked but that was Gary, and he still managed to perform to a great level of consistency over the course of those games.

The Edinburgh derby is one that will always hold fond memories for me as a manager and player. I was lucky to have such a great record against Hibs losing just once against them.

My first derby was at Tynecastle. It came on 27 October 1984 and it was a pretty lifeless 0–0 affair, although I almost turned out to be an instant Hibs hero. I was still on a high after scoring on my debut against Morton but I almost undid all that good early work by giving a horrendous back pass to goalkeeper Henry Smith. It was suicidal play and the ball was intercepted by Micky Weir, but Henry managed to come off his line and make a great block to save my blushes. That was the start of a very good run for me in the Edinburgh derby, I was just relieved we had taken a point.

My opening visit to Easter Road, as a Hearts player, was special. We won 2–1 on New Year's Day, 1985. Gary Mackay put us ahead and I netted our winner. It is fair to say that you would have been lucky if anybody could have caught Gary after his goal. My strike wasn't the best, just a routine striker's finish, but it was to be massive in terms of my Hearts career. I think that goal all but guaranteed my hero status amongst the Tynecastle faithful and it gave me a great feeling. It wasn't until I met the fans and other people in the weeks after that I realised just how important that win was. That feeling for me was second to none, being able to give the fans a genuine feeling of joy and happiness. Hibs did score through Willie Jamieson but it was nothing more than a consolation.

I also managed to get on the scoresheet in the final derby of that 1984–85 season. The match was on 2 April at Tynecastle and we should have left Hibs dead and buried. We went two up, through John Robertson and myself, but Hibs fought back to get a 2–2 draw, thanks to a late double from Joe McBride. Credit to Hibs, they did show a bit of spirit, and there were never any genuinely easy games against them. Come the final whistle of this match if felt more like a defeat, Alex MacDonald had a right go at us after it and rightly so. We still finished above Hibs that season and our record in the derby was probably the difference between the two sides.

The 1985–86 season was another successful one for the maroon side of the city. We opened up with a 2–1 home win at the end of August. I netted the winner that day and I still remember it well. Alan Rough was the Hibs goalkeeper and I loved playing against him because he hated physical confrontation. He was a good goalkeeper but let's just say I never thought he was the bravest. My goal was quite unusual because, as most of my former teammates will confirm, I wasn't exactly blessed with lightning pace. In this match there was a ball over the top, I took Gordon Rae for pace and it should have been a fifty/fifty challenge between Alan and me to get the ball. I managed to get to the ball before Alan, who didn't fancy it, and he left such a massive gap to the side of him that I rolled the ball into the net. It turned out to be the difference between the teams after John

Colquhoun had opened the scoring and Gordon Durie had equalised for Hibs. It was good to get the goal because after that I was forced to start my three-match ban after my now infamous Ibrox clash with Ally McCoist.

The Easter Road outfit had me to thank for getting away with a 0–0 draw that September. I have to hold my hands up and say I should have won us that match. I had a chance at the back post that I should have buried but I pulled my shot wide. That was the season where we came so close to winning the league.

I think every Hearts player could go back to one moment in that season and think if they had done something differently then we might have won the league. My mind always goes back to that chance because if we had won then we could well have ended up being crowned champions. I don't think I missed many chances that season but that was probably one of the easiest. Neil Berry also hit the bar and, all in all, it was a game to forget for all concerned.

The next derby encounter on the first day of 1986 was far more memorable for everyone connected with Hearts, so much so that the Tynecastle faithful composed a song about it:

> First of January Eighty-Six
> Iain slammed one between the sticks
> Robbo too and Sandy Clark
> We're the Gorgie Jam Tarts

We went ahead and John Robertson shocked everyone that day in the build-up to our opener. He went to take a free kick and instead of hitting it, like he normally did, he laid it off to Iain Jardine, who hammered it home. 'Wee Robbo' wasn't to be denied, however, and scored with a volley from a Kenny Black cross. He showed great technique to produce such an exquisite finish. I then scored the third, after a decent passing move. It was a good team goal to put the gloss on a great 3–1 win.

The last derby of that season saw us win 2–1 at Easter Road on 23 March, 1986. I netted the opener where, once again, I found myself staring into the whites of Alan Rough's eyes. I beat him to the ball and stuck it into the net. Steve Cowan levelled for Hibs before John Robertson got our winner from the penalty spot, after Calum Milne had handled on the line. Calum was one of the Hibs player who took defeat badly but we always managed to channel that aggression to our advantage.

The season after we missed out on the double was a sore one, The Hibs fans celebrated our demise almost as much as the Celtic supporters. I think there was even an Albert Kidd Supporters Club named after that Dens Park game, but whether it was the Hibs or Celtic fans I don't know and don't care because it is a club I will never set foot in. That cheap shot certainly didn't hurt or annoy me any more than the events which saw us lose the title on that final day. It is there whenever I talk about Hearts. I don't need anybody else to remind me.

Alex MacDonald certainly gave us a rousing team talk going into that first derby of the 1986–87 season, although we didn't need much motivation with everything that had gone on before. There had been a number of disparaging comments that had come from the Hibs camp after we had lost the league but that only fired us up to get one over our rivals. We had to wait until 30 August to make that first trip across the capital. I got the opener when I got on the end of Gary Mackay's cross and then Iain Jardine and John Robertson scored. Joe McBride got no more than a consolation for Hibs in our 3–1 win – that was a bitter-sweet day.

After the game I remember Alex was really fired up and sparked a sing-song of 'Can you hear the Hibees sing? No, No.' Alex was up banging the wall and everything. He even ordered the team to keep the away dressing room door open until we had finished our sing-song. We proved a point on and off the pitch that day.

We kept our unbeaten run going with a 1–1 draw at Tynecastle in the November meeting. Joe McBride put Hibs in front before Gary Mackay equalised from the penalty spot. I remember I thought to myself, 'Is Gary the right person to take this?' Not because he wasn't a good spot-kick taker but because we all knew, as a Hearts fan, what the derby meant to him. Sometimes you can let your emotions get the better of you but, to be fair to Gary, he stuck it away well and gave Alan Rough no chance. There wasn't much between the teams that day. A draw was probably the right result on a day where Alan Rough had one of his more inspiring days. He made good saves from Wayne Foster and myself to safeguard a point for Hibs. The good thing for us was that it kept our unbeaten run going.

We had to share the spoils again in our first meeting of 1987. That day Hibs played really well against us. They went in front through George McCluskey and it took two brilliant strikes from John Colquhoun to get us something. They were long-range efforts and were as good as I have seen in any game. Those goals put us in front, probably against the run of play, before Mickey Weir equalised for Hibs. We were probably a bit fortunate and had to dig in for a point in that 2–2 draw at Easter Road.

There was no such mistake in the last Tynecastle clash of the 1986–87 season as we beat Hibs 2–1 that April. My big pal Alan Rough gifted us the opener when he spilled a Kenny Black free kick and Roddy MacDonald put the ball into the net. Roddy was something like 25:1 to score the first goal but the bookmaker's definitely missed at least two or three zeros out of those odds. You would have got better odds on Hibs beating Hearts in that period. Roddy then tried to give Hibs a lifeline when he scored an own goal, after a mix-up with Henry Smith. He was lucky I was there to bail him out. The Hibs defender Graham Mitchell made a mistake and I managed to cash in and beat Alan Rough to make sure the points remained at Tynecastle.

We seemed to be unstoppable and we just kept rolling on. John Robertson's goal was enough to give us a 1–0 win in the first meeting of the 1987–88 season. 'Wee Robbo' may have had tendencies towards Hibs when he was younger but there was no questioning his commitment to the Hearts' cause when he pulled on that maroon and white jersey. His scoring record against them was phenomenal, I am sure he must have given Alex Miller a good few sleepless nights. That goal was to mark the last of our unbeaten seventeen-game run against Hibs. It was really great to be part of the team who were involved in the run. The enjoyment that it gave to the fans and ourselves was unbelievable. It is a sequence of results I am proud I was part of and one I will never forget.

Around that time I was beginning to struggle a bit through injury and I wasn't playing as much as before because of my Achilles tendon. I would love to say that was the reason why we finally lost our unbeaten record against Hibs, but they were probably due a result against us. It finally came when they beat us 2–1 at Easter Road on 17 October 1987. All good things have to come to an end at some point. The remaining two fixtures of the 1987–88 season ended goalless. I had to make do with cameo appearances from the bench in those final games in a sign that my playing days were nearing an end.

13

THE HEROES OF HEARTS

THERE ARE so many good players, people and characters that I came across in my time at Tynecastle, and a lot of them I still class as friends today. There are too many to name them all but here are a few I would like to mention.

Alex MacDonald was obviously the manager who signed me for Hearts. 'Wee Doddie' was the undisputed head-tennis king of Hearts, even after he had hung up his boots. We used to play every day in the gym in the old stand at Tynecastle, it was great for young players to improve their touch and technique. 'Doddie' was always the champion, he was incredible and could almost return the ball off any part of his head. His party piece was playing some of the other boys for a signed pound note. He must have a fair collection with a few famous signatures into the bargain. Alex hated to lose at anything, he was just so competitive and that was one of the things that made him such a top player.

Sandy Jardine was Alex's player/assistant before he later stepped up to become co-manager. Playing in the same Hearts team as Sandy was a great experience. His career was amazing, winning thirty-eight Scotland caps along with everything he achieved with Rangers. Sandy, quite rightly, won Scotland's Player of the Year in 1986. He was initially our player assistant before he stepped up to become co-manager with Alex MacDonald. Physically, he never wanted to go into battle but he rarely needed to because he read the game so well. For me, as a professional and the way I played the game, he was amazing. His delivery from defence to the frontline was second to none, the best I have seen. Even today I see very few of the top players who have the quality Sandy had, his right foot was like a golf club. He used to aim for me a lot of the time, as the physical presence in our frontline. It was a ploy we got a lot of joy from, because it enabled John Robertson and John Colquhoun to play off me. I remember speaking to Jimmy Nicholl when he was at Rangers. The opposition all knew what was going to happen but Jimmy admitted they just didn't know how to stop Sandy from picking me out. Some teams tried to put a player in front of me but I knew what areas to go into and if I went there nine times out of ten Sandy would find me, he could put the ball on a sixpence. He was a special talent and his career backs that up. Sandy may have played at the top level but he was also really down to earth and so unassuming. Even when he was combining playing with management he always played to the highest level and he was an absolute delight to play alongside.

When I talk about characters, I can't leave the chairman and owner Wallace Mercer out. Wallace was really passionate about everything he was involved in; I learned a lot from him, good and bad. He was never afraid to have a go and try something. Like a lot of people who get involved in football they become submerged in things and start to forget about the basic principles of business. You see successful people everywhere wanting to get involved in football. They put money up and insist they are going to be sensible but they always get carried away. When they get their foot in the door they lose their head and spend too much money. Wallace was a wee bit like that and went down that road in the pursuit of success. To be fair to him, he never interfered with team affairs although he was probably never allowed because of the strong characters he employed as his managers.

When I was the manager, Wallace loved to have regular chats. I know he used to drive one of my predecessors, Alex MacDonald, mad on that front. Wallace used to go out at lunch time and really enjoy himself. He did all his work in the morning – I think he used to start at the crack of dawn. Afternoons, for him, were to see what was going on in his businesses, including Hearts, but I don't think there was ever a lot of work done. I don't think I am being unfair in saying that because when it came to lunchtime he loved a glass or two of red wine. Every Friday he would come into Tynecastle to talk about the upcoming game. I remember when 'Wee Doddie' was the manager, Walter Borthwick was his assistant and I was the coach, the Tynecastle reception area had a sliding glass window beside the front and people used to go there when they reported to the ground. By the time Friday would come around, the last thing Alex wanted to do was to sit about and talk to Wallace. So 'Wee Doddie' would do everything he could to avoid him. He used to hide in the secretary's office and when he saw Wallace pass the window he would wait a minute then make a mad dash for it, open the window, vault out and race off to his car. He would be away with his car keys and out of Gorgie like a shot. Wallace would then walk into the coaches' room and it would only be Walter, Les Porteous, sometimes Pilmar Smith the vice chairman and myself left. Wallace would come in and ask, 'Where is the manager?' We would have to tell him he had gone. Alex had his routine down to a tee, The Great Houdini could have learned a thing or two from him. 'Wee Doddie' would speak to Wallace when he needed to but when there was nothing to say he wouldn't hang about. He wasn't interested in small talk or general chit-chat. Wallace always wanted to know what was going on and what was happening here and there. Like most business men in football he wanted to get a feel for what was happening at his club.

Alex and Sandy dug out a good few gems for Hearts. One of them was Craig Levein, who they signed from Cowdenbeath. I have never met anyone who was more of natural athlete than Craig. He was so elegant when he ran, the pace he had was incredible and it was such a tragedy that he ended up suffering with such terrible knee injuries.

I played in the game where Craig suffered one of the two horrific knee injuries he had in his career. It happened when we drew 1–1 with Rangers at Tynecastle, I remember scoring the goal but the match will be remembered for Craig doing his cruciate. I had my own problems with my Achilles at the time and I was just pleased that I had scored the goal. It wasn't until I watched the highlights that I realised the extent of Craig's injury. After the game I had been caught up in my own personal glory and that is something I feel really bad about.

It was an absolute tragedy not only for Craig but also for Scottish football because he could have been one of the best defenders this country has ever produced. I am in no doubt he would have moved on to an even bigger club, whether that had been England or the Old Firm I don't know, but teams would have been queuing up to sign him had it not been for his injuries.

Craig is also one of the most intelligent footballers I have come across. He has a very dry sense of humour. When I was manager at Hearts he was my captain and I couldn't praise him enough for the job he did for me. He gave 100 percent in every game and I knew I could rely on him. He was an exemplary captain and whenever he was in my side he always made us a better team.

Craig was unfortunate with injury but the silver lining to that was he was able to start his coaching career a bit earlier than he would have liked. I tried to get him the Hamilton job when he was at Cowdenbeath but that didn't happen. He has since gone on to prove what a top manager he is, first with Hearts, then Leicester City, Raith Rovers, Dundee United and now with the Scottish national team. I am in no doubt Craig is the man who can get Scotland back to the finals of a major tournament again.

My partner-in-crime on the pitch, John Robertson is another Hearts legend. John's goalscoring record at Hearts was second to none. I spent most of my Hearts career playing alongside John and we hardly ever fell out. We knew we could work well together, he was the one with all the natural talent while I had to work hard to achieve everything I did in the game. I might have had to do some extra running or charge into defenders but you knew it was worth it because 'Wee Robbo' would always be there to put the ball in the net and to get us that all-important win bonus. When I bump into John now he still calls me 'Da'. We have always had a mutual respect for one another, he was a top player and because I had a bit more experience I tried to help him along the way.

It didn't matter if it was right foot, left foot or his head, he was absolutely lethal when he got inside that six-yard box. He was just an all-round top footballer. He did get some stick for his weight from time to time, that was totally justified because sometimes he would let himself go, but you knew if he was fighting fit then there were few better finishers in the British game. He is quite rightly seen as a Hearts legend.

The one area where John does let himself down is in his love of statistics and facts. That is how he got his nickname 'Ceefax'. He has got such a wealth of knowledge and could probably tell you every goal he has ever scored. He has an unbelievable memory and could put you to sleep with his eye for detail. John has since put his knowledge to good use and has done well for himself in management at Hearts, Inverness, Ross County, Livingston and East Fife.

When it comes to Hearts there is nobody more passionate about the club than Gary Mackay. He holds the record for the number of competitive appearances for the club. He probably cares about the club too much, wears his heart on his sleeve and always says what he thinks. As a player he was a real talent. People talk about awareness and that is important in football. I knew when Gary stepped onto the pitch where he would run and he also knew what I would do. At times it was almost tele-pathic when he broke from the midfield to support me. Gary was the one who linked the defence to the frontline. Gary was a real character off the pitch too. When he was out with his good pal Kenny Black anything could happen. The pair were dyna-mite together, they would cut ties in the dressing room and nail shoes to the floor. The only time I fell victim to them was when they cut my boxer shorts up. I lost the plot and let's just say nothing like that ever happened to me again.

I am still friends with Gary today. It is sad he has had his disagreements with Vladimir Romanov because I know how much Hearts means to him. The bottom line is he will always do what he feels is in the best interests of the club.

When it comes to goalkeepers Henry Smith would be up there with the best I have played with or against. He was a good shot stopper and he could also kick the ball for miles with his trusty left foot. Henry was a pleasure to play with but he was also a character. We used to joke that he used to have an alter-ego, sometimes he hardly spoke to anyone and the next day he would be the life and soul of the party. I always categorise goalkeepers into two sections – they are really intelligent or stupid. But, I have to say, Henry fools me because I am still not sure where he falls.

You would know what sort of mood Henry was in by the accent he put on that day. He spent a lot of time down south. There were times when he would sound like he had spent all his days down in England and the next he would come in and speak with a bit of a Scottish twang. Henry got a fair bit of stick about that but as a goalkeeper he was top-drawer and a great servant to Hearts. You knew with Henry behind you that you always had a chance because he was capable of pulling off world-class saves, he was that good. He earned a few Scotland caps and, for me, he more than merited them. I am in no doubt he would have got a few more had there not been so many good Scottish goalkeepers on the scene at the same time.

I am sure Henry would also admit that he was helped having a character like Walter Kidd in front of him. Every winger or striker hated playing against Walter. I was close friends with the late Rangers and Scotland star Davie Cooper and whenever we met he would always ask if Walter Kidd would be playing against him. I met him in Hamilton the day before Hearts were due to play Rangers in a game at Tynecastle. Davie said to me, 'Is that head case Jack Nicholson playing right back tomorrow? If he is I'll be playing on our right!' That was Walter, he was your typical no-nonsense defender. He would kick you and keep kicking you, never took any prisoners. He was the ideal man to have in the trenches alongside you, as I found that day when we took on the Rangers team at Ibrox.

He was a real Hearts servant and knew his strengths and his weaknesses. What 'Coop' said pretty much summed Walter up. He played like that against everyone and you knew you were going to be in for a nightmare ninety minutes if you were up against him. He was primarily a defender but was willing to get forward whenever he could. You would get the occasional half-decent cross off him that would give you a chance to score, but that didn't happen too often.

Walter and I got on really well, he was my roommate for most of my time at Hearts. He was the best roommate you could ever ask for. If I couldn't be bothered to get up for breakfast then he would always bring me something back and he was always a top man with an iron in his hand. He would do all my ironing when we were away and everything would be immaculate. We used to go to Walter and Mary's house and he would never let her iron his shirts.

Fellow defender Brian Whittaker was another real character and probably was a shining light to everybody around him. He was just so full of life and loved to have a laugh and a joke about things. Some of the things he got up to were unbelievable but, unfortunately, there would have been no chance of the publisher allowing us to print any of them, outwith his under-cover cop prank and hiding a fish in Roddy MacDonald's car.

As a player he was decent, a good defender, but as a party animal he was world-class. He loved life and he lived it to the full. If you are going to die young then I suppose you might as well make the most of what you have got. The tragedy was that he was only forty when he passed away and it was devastating. Brian died in a car crash and I don't think anybody knows exactly what happened. I classed Brian as a good friend, I had known him a long time, playing with him and against him. His death was a real loss and I remember being at his funeral and it was such a sad, sad day.

I am still friendly with a lot of that Hearts team, including George Cowie. I first met George at West Ham United. His career was cut short through injury but he is now making a real name for himself out in Australia as a coach. He turns up like the bad penny, phoning when he has had a drink and with the time difference I have taken many an early morning call from George wanting to reminisce about the good old days. He was part of that 1985–86 Hearts team and as a player you knew you could always rely on him to give you absolutely everything.

Another Tynecastle icon I must mention is Wayne Foster. I still see 'Fozzie' from time to time and he has never changed, he is still a big, daft Englishman and a real infectious character. Wayne is a postman now in Edinburgh and I think he walks around 100 miles a week. Even that weekly shift wouldn't tire his tongue because he never shuts up. He talks from the moment he gets up until the moment he falls asleep. As a player he was whole-hearted and the goal that will always stick out for me, and every Hearts fan, was the one he got in the Scottish Cup, when he came off the bench, to score the winner against Hibs at Easter Road. That is the one where he runs over and jumps on top of the fence to celebrate with the Hearts fans. That was a big day for us and a really massive result.

14

HOW MUCH FOR THE HIBEES?

AT THE start of the 1987–88 campaign I began to have problems with my Achilles tendon. The tendons in both legs used to tighten up and after some games I could hardly walk. It was a nightmare and things got so bad that the physio, Alan Rae, had to put my ankle in plaster. It immobilised my leg and took the strain off the tendons. We hoped it would help take some of the inflammation away and it worked in the short term. I started to struggle for fitness and spent most of that season on the bench. Personally, it was the campaign from hell, I never really felt fit and I was always in pain, although the good thing was the team, at least, kicked on.

Alex MacDonald also started to change the team about a bit. Mike Galloway came in from Halifax for £60,000, probably to replace me. Mike ended up being a brilliant signing for Hearts and they went on to sell him for over £500,000 to Celtic – it was a decent bit of business from Alex and Sandy. Dave McPherson also arrived from Rangers and proved to be another quality addition. The likes of Henry Smith, John Colquhoun and Gary Mackay also got some long overdue international recognition – with Gary scoring his glory goal against Bulgaria.

I did chip in with a few goals as the team continued to push for the title. We were on top for a spell but, in the end, we had to settle for second spot, to a Celtic team who celebrated their centenary season as champions. The highlight of that campaign for me came off the pitch. I had met my partner Liz a couple of years earlier and we decided it was time to tie the knot. The wedding was great and I couldn't have asked for anything more from Liz and her family. Her dad, George, and her mum, Margaret, were two of the nicest people you could meet, as they took me into their family and treated me like their own son, although, sadly, George is now no longer with us. I also have to mention Liz's two sisters, Marian and Mags. Marian is married to Richard and Mags is hitched to my Moodiesburn drinking partner Danny. When we go through to visit them we normally end up in The Silver Larch, where we have had some great nights and banter in a bar that is very much divided by the Old Firm. Liz and I have now been together for more than twenty-five years. We have had a real solid and strong relationship through that time. Liz has been there for me through all the ups and downs. Liz probably deserves a medal for putting up with me for as long as she has. It is like every marriage, you have your good and bad days but going through them all helps make the relationship stronger. I have now mastered the art of a good marriage – I now accept that all the problems and issues are down to me. All joking aside, I would not be where I am without her. I think once you strip things away in football you can count your genuine friends on both hands. What I can say is Liz has been my best friend over the last twenty-five years. Our first son, Gary Robert George Clark, arrived on 29 May 1988. I would like to put it on the record that Liz was responsible for the length of his name, I was perfectly happy with Gary Clark but Liz wanted to put in the middle names after both our dads. I remember when we were over in Disneyland, Florida, on holiday. An American woman asked two-year-old Gary what his name was, and he replied, 'Gary Robert George Clark.' The American just looked at him and laughed and said, 'I think we should be naming a building after you.'

Just before Gary was born one of my surrogate sons in football, John Robertson, decided it was time to move on. He was sold to Newcastle United and it allowed us to bring in Iain Ferguson and Eammon Bannon from Dundee United. It was all change going into the 1988–89 season and, for me, it was the beginning of the end. I ended up snapping my Achilles tendon in my left leg and I was still having problems with my right leg as well. The tendon went in our League Cup win over Meadowbank Thistle. I had been in chronic pain with the injury, despite the best efforts of Alan Rae, and it just snapped during that game. It was 23 August 1988 at Brockville Stadium. I just collapsed in pain, as it went. Ironically, not long before that Alan and I had agreed I would go in for an operation, but we had decided to put it off until after our European games against the Irish side, St Patrick's. I didn't get that far and basically my first-team career at Hearts was all but over. It was down to a combination of the injury and the fact I was in my early thirties, nearing the end of my career.

The good thing, from my point of view, was that I had started my SFA coaching badges and at least had them to fall back on. I was also fortunate that the chairman, Wallace Mercer, decided it was time for a change. Alex MacDonald and Sandy Jardine were co-managers but Wallace didn't feel things were going as well as they should have been. Wallace ended up sacking Sandy and left the job to Alex, meaning his first-team coach Walter Borthwick had to step up. I still don't know to this day why Sandy was sacked but it left a void in our backroom staff. Alex asked me if I would help out and do some coaching by taking the reserves. Alex knew I was probably not going to play again and gave me the opportunity to start out on my coaching career. I have to say I am eternally grateful to Alex because you need to start somewhere and he gave me a fantastic opportunity, at a club that meant so much to me.

When I was asked to give something back and get involved with coaching the reserves and youths I didn't have to be asked twice. I knew I was entering the twilight of my career and coaching was the next logical step and something I had a real passion for – although I remained registered as a player.

It was not long after that I got to meet one of my football heroes, Pele. The Brazilian legend was over in Scotland to help do some promotional work for the FIFA under-16 World Championship. That was the competition where Scotland, who boasted the likes of Paul Dickov, Brian O'Neil and Gary Bollan, got to the final and eventually lost out to Saudi Arabia. The semi-final between Scotland and Portugal was played at Tynecastle and Pele was there to watch the game. It was a real night to remember in front of a sell-out crowd and to meet one of the true greats of the world game, while also watching the young Scots win 1–0 thanks to an O'Neil goal. That Scotland team did the nation proud before they eventually lost to Saudi Arabia in the final.

It was while I was away with a young Hearts team I faced the nightmare scenario that no SFA coaching course can prepare you for. I was across in Croix, France, with Walter Borthwick. We had been invited to play in the prestigious French youth tournament at the end of the 1989–90 season. I was in my hotel room finalising the training for that afternoon when the telephone rang. I picked up the receiver and Wallace Mercer was on the line. That was nothing unusual but I will never forget the next thing he said to me. He said, 'Sandy, I want you to put a valuation on every player in the Hibs first team. I want you to give me a rough estimate of their individual values because I am trying to buy Hibs.' I remember being on the line and I just stood there shaking my head, I was in a state of shock, I couldn't believe what Wallace had just told me. My initial reaction was that it was a wind-up, but you knew when it came to Wallace that anything was possible. Wallace always liked to make headlines and do things differently. To this day, I don't know if he was genuinely intent on buying Hibs or if it was just a massive publicity stunt. If it was a PR stunt then it certainly worked a treat because it put him on the front page of every national newspaper in Scotland and at the top of every news bulletin when the story broke. It also made Wallace one of the most talked about men in Scottish football.

I was waiting for Wallace to phone me back and tell me it was one of those radio wind-ups. I then went and spoke to Walter who confirmed he had also had a similar conversation with Wallace. We both just looked at each other in disbelief and joked has Wallace finally lost the plot? We didn't think for a minute it would happen but we both agreed we'd better do what he had asked – he was our boss after all. So we both got a piece of paper and made a list of all the Hibs players and then put a valuation beside each one of them. I have to admit my valuations weren't too high on any of them. If I am being honest, I didn't rate many of them, we only lost to them once during my playing days and they were always second-best when it came to the derbies. They couldn't beat us or get a result against us for love nor money. The Hibs teams weren't in the same class as the Hearts sides I played in, every single one of their teams lacked something. Put it this way, if I had been a Premier League manager then I wouldn't have been chapping at the Easter Road front door looking to sign any of them. I think my valuations ranged from £20,000 to £120,000, which were reasonable prices, although I think Walter maybe rated one or two of their players slightly higher than I did.

We both put the values of our Hibs squad together and gave them to the secretary, Les Porteous, when we arrived back at Tynecastle. He passed them on to Wallace and then he could put them together and get a rough average. Wallace was looking to get values so he could gauge what their squad was worth and make sure he wasn't paying over the odds. There would have been no chance of Wallace giving them more than market value. Putting values on the Hibs players was the only involvement I had in proceedings and in all honesty I thought that would be the last I would hear of Wallace's madcap idea.

A couple of weeks later the story broke in the press that Wallace was looking to buy Hibs. He even held a press conference in an Edinburgh hotel to outline his plans. I remember it being all over the papers and the news, with Wallace in his element in the middle of every photograph. Wallace went on to outline his grand master plan, claiming it would be in the interests of Edinburgh and Scottish football in general. He wanted to amalgamate Hearts and Hibs under the guise of Edinburgh United. He also claimed he was looking to move the new team to a new purpose-built stadium on the outskirts of the city. It was a bold plan – others might call it crazy. Wallace felt together Hearts and Hibs would be stronger and would be able to compete with the Old Firm. He also said he had canvassed opinion from the capital's business fraternity and there was massive support for an Edinburgh United. It is fair to say the Hearts or Hibs fans didn't share his vision or his enthusiasm for his capital dream. Hearts fans were unhappy but that was nothing compared to the anger that was vented by the Hibs support – who claimed the move wouldn't be a merger but a takeover.

I still had my doubts but Wallace was doing a good job of

selling his daring plan to anyone who would listen. I was starting to think maybe Wallace might pull this off after all, although at the back of my head I knew there was no way it could happen. Knowing Wallace, as I did, it probably started off as a bit of a pipedream but once the story gathered pace and he saw he was getting loads of exposure and publicity then I am sure that would have driven him on. It also helped his position that Hibs were in a financial mess. The companies who owned Hibernian were in a bit of debt and that opened the door for Wallace.

The Hibs support were utterly disgusted and bitterly opposed to the move, who could blame them? They were furious and made their feelings known. I think most of them would rather have seen Hibs fold than fall into the hands of Wallace Mercer; to them Wallace was the devil – wearing a Hearts scarf. They got a protest group up and running and that was where the 'Hands off Hibs' campaign was born. They made it their aim to save their club and were prepared to do it by any means possible.

I am sure if it had been the other way round the Hearts fans would have done exactly the same. I am certain every Jambo would have got together to make sure that their club didn't fall into the hands of Hibs. There are just too many strong Hibs and Hearts supporters around for something like that to happen. The Hibs fans staged huge fundraisers and massive protest rallies, supported by the musical combo The Proclaimers and boyhood fan Gordon Strachan, as they tried to fight off the threat of Hibernian being wiped off the face of Scottish football.

Legends like Pat Stanton and our own striker John Robertson also attended a rally decrying Mercer. It is well known that John grew up watching Hibs on the terraces of Easter Road. I think we managed to convert him a little bit during his time at Tynecastle, but I don't think his true feelings for Hibs ever went away – even though he did more damage to them as a player than anybody else in white and maroon. I know John was totally against the idea of a united Edinburgh team. He made his feelings clear in and around the club whenever anybody asked him about the possible merger.

Wallace was dubbed Wallace Mercer-nary by the Hibs support. A petition was handed in to Number 10 Downing Street, when the Conservative Party's Margaret Thatcher was the Prime Minister. Wallace certainly caused a stir to say the least. Things also turned quite ugly at times, Mercer's children had to be escorted to school while he and his wife, Anne, both received death threats. Bricks and boulders were also thrown through the windows of Wallace's offices, while his cars had to be regularly checked for bombs. It was scary stuff although I genuinely don't believe any of the Hibs fans would actually have harmed Wallace or any of his family. Obviously, when Wallace and his family were threatened the police had to take the threats seriously. I don't think you can ever take anything like that too lightly. I also don't think the Lothian and Borders Police were too happy with the situation either, as there must have been a few overtime claims put in, as Wallace and his family were put under twenty-four-hour surveillance.

Wallace ended up gaining more than sixty percent of the shares from Edinburgh Hibernian PLC but it still wasn't enough to secure the majority share he needed to claim control. The Hibs chairman David Duff effectively killed the move when he refused to sell his eleven percent stake. If he had agreed then Wallace would have got the shares he needed, but instead it was another Edinburgh businessman that turned out to be the white knight of Easter Road. The former Kwik Fit tycoon Tom Farmer, who had a family connection with the Leith club, was persuaded by the 'Hands off Hibs' campaign to come in and invest the money that was needed to keep the club afloat. The 'Hands off Hibs' campaign probably saved their club. Once they got Farmer on board that all but ended Wallace's hopes. I think Wallace also knew at that point his dream had been crushed. Wallace released a statement saying he had decided to drop his interest because the remainder of the Hibs board wouldn't sell their shares and his business advisors were also concerned that the financial position at Hibs was worse than they had feared. At the end of the day, Wallace's bold bid didn't come off but it will never be forgotten. It was a headline-grabbing move and one that will go down in Scottish football history and one that Wallace will be forever remembered for.

Wallace's probably ended up helping Hibs more than Hearts with that whole saga. I think what happened and the fact that Hibs had come so close to disappearing rejuvenated our Edinburgh rivals. If I am being honest I wouldn't have liked to see Hibs and Hearts disappear for a united Edinburgh team. I think that would have been a bad move for Scottish football. I think our game would be far poorer without Hearts and Hibs. I also don't think it would have ever worked out, as I firmly believe Wallace would have lost a lot of supporters from both sides if his grand plan had come to fruition. They are both institutions and are stronger because of each other. They are rivals but they also need each other.

15

NO THRILLS AT FIRHILL

I JOKE that this period in my managerial career was 'my weekend away' because it didn't last long at all. I can look back and laugh at things now because my time as manager of Partick Thistle was a bit of a nightmare. It was my first move into frontline management and by my own admission it was a total disaster. To be fair, I had been advised against taking the job by Alex MacDonald, Les Porteous and Wallace Mercer. They all told me that they felt the offer had come too early in my managerial career. I had just turned thirty-three and was just coming to the end of my playing career. I listened to what they had to say and took their advice on board but it still had to be my decision and I thought I knew better. I felt Partick Thistle was a good club, they were well positioned in the First Division, sitting second in the league, and I believed I could do well at Firhill and get them promotion to the Scottish Premier Division.

There was also a bit of a personal pull to the Thistle job as well. The initial approach came from my former Airdrie manager Bobby Watson who was on the board with the chairman Jim Donald. John Lambie had left to manage Hamilton Accies and Bobby called me and asked if I would be interested in the job. I went and spoke to them and they offered me the post. I knew they were only part-time and it would be like going back to my

old Airdrie days, but I still believed it was too good an opportunity to turn down. The chairman had big plans for Thistle and
sold them to me. Jim told me at that initial meeting how he
planned to sell off some of the ground around Firhill for flats
and re-invest it in the club. It never happened in my time, although
in all seriousness I wasn't there long enough for much to happen,
although it did eventually come to fruition a bit further down
the line. I had a good feeling from that first meeting with Jim
and I obviously knew Bobby Watson well and could trust him
implicitly. If I hadn't known Bobby and got on so well with Jim
then I might have had second thoughts, but I had absolutely no
doubts and agreed to take the job.

I decided to take Iain Jardine in as my No. 2. He had played
with me at Hearts and also had had a spell at Thistle. It is probably a decision, looking back, that I regret. It had nothing to do
with appointing Iain or his abilities as an assistant manager but
with the way his return tarnished his reputation with the Thistle
faithful. Iain found it hard. He got stick from the fans because
he left them first time around as a player and then he got it in
the neck again when our Thistle team started to struggle. Iain
ended up on the bandwagon of things that were going wrong
for me. He was a victim of circumstances and I feel a sense of
guilt that Iain was dragged into things because he was only
guilty through association.

I realised I was in for a rude awakening from day one. It was
hard making the switch back to working primarily with part-
time players. There were also a lot of strong characters in that
Firhill dressing room, guys like Chic Charnley, who was the only
full-time senior professional at the club, the rest of the squad
was made up of YTS players. I know Chic had a wayward reputation but I have to say he was great to work with, he had unbelievable ability and was brilliant in my time at Thistle. He was

112

really easy to manage and gave me absolutely everything he had out on the pitch. Gerry Collins was another stalwart of the former Partick Thistle boss John Lambie, but he was also different class for me. He tried everything he could to get the best out of the players and, like myself, couldn't quite put his finger on why things didn't click.

My first game was a 1–1 draw at Raith Rovers. We then beat Hamilton and Meadowbank and drew with Airdrie, so in the first four games we were unbeaten but after that we couldn't buy a win. We went into freefall and couldn't get out of the rut. I also knew things weren't quite right behind the scenes. I was aware there were issues but I didn't realise just how destabilising they were going to be. The main one was that the former manager, John Lambie, still had the ear of most of my players. Some of the boys even told me they had been speaking to John, and he had made it clear to them that he wasn't happy at Hamilton and was desperate to return to Thistle. John had managed and signed most of them, so I suppose the players felt they owed him a degree of loyalty. They enjoyed working with him and naturally if they thought there was a chance they could get him back then they would do whatever they could to make it happen. Looking back, I don't think all the players at Firhill could look me in the eye and say they gave me absolutely everything. I know for a fact that there were one or two who were working well within their capabilities. They were doing the minimum in training and in matches – it was clear they were never going to bust a gut for me. I was still working away and doing what I believed to be the right thing, getting the team organised and ready for a Saturday, but the confidence drained by the game and we had well and truly come off the rails. During that dreadful run we played Aberdeen in the third round of the Scottish Cup, we got thumped 6–2 at Firhill and it was an afternoon to forget

– for my team and me. I got sent to the stands and ended up getting hit with a lengthy touchline ban from the Scottish Football Association. The referee, Dougie Hope, in my opinion, had been a total joke. He had given a couple of debatable penalties against us and I ended up slaughtering him and telling him what I thought of his sub-standard performance, so he sent me off. I got a three-month touchline ban that didn't help my cause in trying to turn things around at Thistle.

I started to get a lot of stick from the fans. It was hardly a surprise, I totally understood where they were coming from. Every football supporter wants to see their team winning and if they don't then they get frustrated and end up venting their feelings at the players or more often than not the manager. It isn't very pleasant when you are the one in the firing line, but it is part and parcel of the job. Every manager knows it is a pitfall of the job when they sign on that dotted line. The abuse should never be taken as a personal slur. I don't think the Thistle fans disliked me as a person, but they hated the way I was managing their club. Once you lose the fans there is normally only one outcome and the disgruntled Thistle punters didn't have to wait too long to get me out the door.

We were ahead at my old club Airdrie and ended up losing 3–2. I knew then the end was near and sure enough it came when we lost 1–0 away to Alloa in the following game. The chairman, Jim Donald, pulled me in after that defeat and told me he had to make the change. To be fair to the chairman, he was genuinely upset with the way things had turned out. I had no complaints about his decision, he had to do what was best for Partick Thistle and there was still a chance they could get back into the promotion chase. I also knew in my heart of hearts that I wasn't going to turn things around. If I am being honest, I probably felt relieved when the situation was taken out of my hands. Our results hadn't been good and we were nowhere near the promotion places. The split was pretty amicable and I got every penny of my contract paid up without the slightest problem. The club dealt with everything professionally and I shook hands with the directors before I left and wished them all the best. We parted on good terms and I was just disappointed that things hadn't turned out differently for the team and myself.

I was devastated with the way my first venture into management had panned out. Wallace Mercer, Alex MacDonald and Les Porteous had been right, I wasn't experienced enough to handle such a high-profile first job. My inexperience ended up being my downfall. I was naive and didn't recognise that my players weren't giving everything they had in games and because of that I probably picked the wrong team at times. I was maybe a bit wet behind the ears. I have always tried to be honest throughout my entire career and life, I believe that is very important, but I don't know if all my Thistle players were as honest and up front with me. They certainly weren't hurting as much as me after we had lost games. It took me a while to find out where this was coming from and by the time I did it was too late. It was a harsh lesson I was forced to learn and one I was never going to let happen again in management. I think after that I could sense if players were with me or not.

It was also hardly a surprise Partick Thistle decided to replace me with John Lambie. I didn't have a problem with the board's decision. If they felt John was the man to change their fortunes then who was I to argue? I also have to state on the record that I don't blame John for what happened to me. It was still my job to get results, regardless of what was going on in the dressing room or behind the scenes, and my team and I weren't getting results. John sensed he had made a mistake by going to Hamilton and realised that if I continued to struggle then maybe the door would open for him again at Partick Thistle. You have to give John credit because he worked the situation to his advantage and got the job he wanted after I left, and it certainly proved to be a success. I think history shows that John Lambie and Partick Thistle fit like hand in glove, John has had so much success there. He did brilliantly for the club and is quite rightly seen as a legendary figure in the history of Partick Thistle.

In lots of ways I regret taking the Thistle job, but on a number of levels it had been a great learning curve and a real crash-course to first-team management. The low points and difficult times I went through at Firhill are things I have been able to look back on and use to my advantage in subsequent manage-rial jobs. I had my SFA coaching badges and played football at a high level so I thought I was ready to walk into management. What happened at Firhill made me a better person and more prepared for the future. You learn more about life and yourself in difficult situations and in adversity than when things are going well. That was definitely the case when I look back at my time at Partick Thistle. Daft as it sounds, it was probably the best thing that ever happened to me.

After I left Firhill I decided to get the boots back on. I played a few times at Thistle but I had focused primarily on the manage-ment side. Iain Munro, who was co-manager at Dunfermline with Jim Leishman, asked me if I would go and help them out. They had just returned to the Scottish Premier Division and he felt my experience could help them in their bid for survival. I knew Iain from doing my SFA coaching badges with him down at Largs and he asked if I would come in and play a couple of trial matches. I played a game against Celtic reserves and things went well, my fitness was still decent. I wasn't at the peak of my playing career but I knew I could still do a job so I signed a short-term deal with Dunfermline. I didn't want anything long term because I knew my old job was waiting for me back at Hearts. Alex MacDonald had already told me I would be coming back as his reserve team coach but he wanted to leave it for a few months before I returned. I think he was worried how things might have been perceived if I had walked out of Firhill and straight back to Tynecastle. It wouldn't have bothered me in the slightest but I was still more than happy to sit tight and wait my time. I shook hands on a deal with Iain Munro and the deal was that if, or when, they had enough points on the board and they were safe then I would rip up my contract and return to Hearts. It was an agreement that suited everybody. Iain also did me a favour employing me as a player-coach and that allowed me to eat into my SFA ban that was hanging over me from my time at Firhill.

I ended up playing four games for the Pars, it was a good pick-me-up after everything that had happened at Thistle. It was great to be back in a dressing room environment because for the first time in my life I had been sitting in the house doing nothing and feeling a bit sorry for myself. Dunfermline also had a decent bunch of lads and team as well. Jimmy Nicholl was there, the Hungarian Istvan Kosma, Paul Smith and also the captain of the side was the late Norrie McCathie. I also played a couple of games upfront with a young Northern Irish player that went by the name of George O'Boyle. He was an exceptional little striker but at that time I had no idea of the problems he was going to cause me later in my managerial career, although at that point all I had to do was concentrate on playing.

Jim Leishman and Iain Munro were the co-managers who were charged with keeping Dunfermline up. Everybody in football knows how Jim works, and in my six weeks at Dunfermline I don't think I saw him at training once as he left everything on the football side to Iain. Iain did all the training, tactics and set pieces, etc. Jim was away doing whatever Jim did. 'Leish' was a great figurehead for Dunfermline, he is an icon at East End Park but don't ask me what he is like as a coach because I have absolutely no idea. To be fair it was a partnership that both Jim and Iain were happy with and who could argue with it because it certainly brought great success to Dunfermline.

We lost in my first game against Dundee United and also against Hearts but I played in wins against Motherwell and St Mirren that were enough to keep Dunfermline up with two games to go. I left on a high knowing that I had helped play my part in keeping Dunfermline up. It also meant that I didn't have to wait until the end of the season to make my emotional return to Hearts and Tynecastle. It was the perfect end to what had hardly been the ideal season.

16

ALL GOOD THINGS MUST COME TO AN END

I WAS quite happy working away in the background continuing to learn the ropes of management, although that all changed when Wallace decided to sack Alex MacDonald in September 1990, after we lost to Rangers. I was devastated for him, having worked under him as a player and coach, because I genuinely felt there was nobody better qualified to do the job. I didn't think there was much of a problem at the club but Wallace obviously viewed things differently. But, as I know, getting sacked doesn't necessarily mean you're a bad manager. I am sure it was a sad day for Wallace when he made that call because over the previous ten years they had had a good chairman/manager relationship. They weren't the best of friends but they did work well together. Alex deserves a lot of credit for the job he did at Hearts. When he took over the club were in a right mess and he built them up and into one of the most competitive clubs in Scotland. When the news leaked out that Alex and Walter Borthwick had left everybody at the club was totally devastated. It left us with nobody on the coaching staff because our other coach John Binnie, who was only part-time, was very close to Alex and he tendered his resignation on hearing the news. I was the only one left and so Wallace asked me if I would take temporary charge, until he appointed a new manager. I went and spoke to Alex before I made a decision. I was in a difficult position because I still had a young family to support and couldn't afford to just walk away from the club in support of Alex.

The first thing I did after I had that conversation with Wallace was to drive to Kirkintilloch to see Alex. I couldn't find him at first because his wife, Christine, informed me that he was away playing tennis. I eventually tracked him down at the local tennis court. I had to go and see Alex, he had helped me a lot as a player and a coach and I was genuinely disappointed to see him go. Alex, as always, was philosophical and met the setback of being sacked head on. We had a chat and he told me that it would be a good experience for me to take temporary charge of Hearts. I felt a bit better taking the job knowing that I had Alex's backing.

I then had to turn my attentions to my first managerial challenge at Hearts – a baptism of fire in the Edinburgh derby. I had plenty of experience as a player but suddenly I was this rookie manager in the firing line for a match at Easter Road. I was still quite young and Wallace wasn't quite sure if I could handle it myself. He was a wee bit worried that I might struggle with the demands and pressures so he brought my former Rangers manager Jock Wallace in, in an advisory capacity. To be fair to him, he never interfered once. All he said to me was, 'Are you okay? Do you know what you are doing?' I had done all my preparations and I was happy with everything. He just shook my hand and wished me all the best and said he was there if I needed to turn to him.

I had always been lucky against Hibs as a player and, thankfully, that good fortune followed me into management. I made a few minor tweaks to Alex's team but nothing major. I brought Jimmy Sandison in as a sweeper and young George Wright in, who had done well for me in the reserves. Things couldn't have gone any better and we went in at the interval 3–0 up, with goals from Craig Levein and a John Robertson double. The Hibs fans were so annoyed at their team that some of them invaded the pitch and tried to get the game abandoned. The referee took us off the pitch but thankfully the police and stewards managed to restore the peace and we were able to resume.

The main problem for me that day was I was still banned from the touchline, as a result of the SFA ban I had been hit with at Partick Thistle. I was sitting in the stands and had to leave David McCreery, who was an experienced Northern Irish midfielder but was out injured, on the bench with Bert Logan. We had walkie-talkies but I also needed a runner and there was nobody better suited for that job than our fitness coach George McNeill – a former world sprint champion. At 1–0 I wanted to make a wee change to our formation, I asked George to go down to the bench and get McCreery to get our right wing back, Wright, to sit a bit more. George jumped up and ran down the stairs but by the time he got to the dugout we had scored again and he had forgotten what he had to say. So he turned to McCreery and said, 'Sandy has said we have to try and score a third!' George came back up and then asked me what he was meant to have said. Both George and Bert were great people to have about the club and that was all down to the spirit and togetherness that Alex MacDonald had nurtured at the club.

Also, because of the ban, I didn't realise that I wasn't allowed to go on the pitch before the game. I thought I was only banned from the touchline during the game and so I went out and put the team through their warm-up. It wasn't as if we had many other options on the coaching front! Sure enough, the well-respected journalist and television presenter Gerry McNee phoned me on the Sunday to tell me that one of his fellow professionals had reported me to the Scottish Football Association for being on the pitch. And people wonder why I have reservations about certain members of the written press. Thankfully, Gerry agreed to do me a favour and got *Scotsport* to drop the footage from their programme. That meant the SFA couldn't take action against me because they had no proof I had been out on the pitch. I was pleased that it was the team who took all the headlines and not me after the game. The response the players gave and the way they played showed me that Alex should never have been sacked.

I had to go out on a spy trip to Dnipro, in the Ukraine, just before Alex left. That turned out being a nightmare journey. I went out with Ian Dunwoody, who was the managing director of Travel Management, the official travel agent for the club. Travelling to the Ukraine, prior to the break-up of the Eastern Bloc, was a bit of a challenge, starting with my travel documentation. After that was sorted we flew from London to Moscow. We then thought we would fly to the Ukraine but we had to make that trip by overnight train. We were told it would take twelve hours by train and then another three by car. We decided we would go to the train station early to have a few beers and that would help us sleep through the journey but unknown to us there was a ban on alcohol being sold in public places so we had to make the entire trip stone-cold sober. We eventually made it to the Ukraine about seven am the next morning and then we had to travel, rather suspiciously, in two separate cars to Dnipro. It was an interesting journey to say the least. Once we got there everything was fine and the locals gave us the best of food and everything and, if I am being honest, they were probably taking it off their own plates to feed us. I felt really bad because it was clear the locals didn't have much. When we got to the ground we asked their club officials why we hadn't flown from Moscow and they told us we had to go this way to make sure we made the game because the Russian authorities at that time used to cancel flights to the Ukraine all the time and they feared we might be left stranded in the Russian capital.

The Ukraine might have been a poor country but it was clear when it came to football they had an abundance of riches, that Dnipro side were a really good team. The good news was that we were allowed to get a direct flight back to Moscow.

It was just as well I made that trip because the UEFA Cup clash in Dnipro was one of the games where I had to keep the manager's hot-seat warm. John Robertson scored a header to put us in front then they equalised through Yuriy Hudymenko and, in the end, we were left holding on because they absolutely battered us. It was a good result for the team, against a really talented side. I returned to Edinburgh airport to be greeted by Wallace Mercer, who was there to tell me that Joe Jordan was to be appointed as Hearts manager the next day. Joe was great and he came in but he was wise because he kept me in charge for the next game which was against Celtic. We lost 3–0, but we didn't play badly, we were a bit jet-lagged and heavy-legged after our European adventure and Joe had maybe seen that. I was more than delighted to have got my first taste of being in charge at Hearts. It was a great experience but I was more than happy to return to my role with the youth and reserve teams. I got on with the job in hand of trying to bring through more youngsters for Joe's first team and also keeping his other fringe players ticking over. Joe did reasonably well in his first season at Hearts, finishing in fifth place in the Scottish Premier Division. There were definite signs of progress.

The youth ranks of the Clark family were also boosted that summer. Liz and I welcomed our second son, Nicky. He was born on 3 June 1991. From an early age Nicky only ever wanted to play football. He used to hate going to school. Liz picked up a clearly unhappy boy after school one day. Nicky asked, 'Why do I need to go to school?' Liz said, 'So you can learn new things every day.' Nicky replied, 'What is the point in spending six hours at school? Can I not just stay at home and practise my free kicks?'

17

HELPING TO UNLOCKE SOME
MAGICAL TYNECASTLE TALENT

MY FORMER Hearts teammate Eammon Bannon had not long
been appointed assistant manager of Hearts to Tommy McLean
when he claimed his newly-inherited squad would never do
anything because they didn't have any decent young players
coming through the ranks. It was at the start of the 1994–95
season after I had just been sacked as manager, although I will
go into that later. There is always a lot of rubbish spouted in
football but Eammon's comments, for me, took the biscuit. It
was so wide of the mark it was untrue. I couldn't believe it when
I heard what Eammon had said. I had expected better, especially
as I had played alongside him and he had strong connections
with Hearts. Eammon had come through the Tynecastle ranks
before he moved to Chelsea and later returned for a second spell
in Gorgie.

I have to say that Eammon's comments more than got under
my skin. Everyone is entitled to their opinion but I just couldn't
believe what he had said, because nothing could have been further
from the truth. I had been involved with coaching the kids at
Tynecastle over the previous six years, outwith my short spells
at Partick Thistle and Dunfermline, and that was the one area
of the club where I knew there was genuine talent and hope for

the future. A number of the youth players, like Paul Ritchie, Allan Johnston and Gary Locke, had already broken through into the first team. They all did it in some style, starring for Hearts before they moved on to pastures new, although it was no thanks to McLean and Bannon, who decided to go for more experience. It wasn't until Jim Jefferies came in that they really began to flourish. Ritchie and Johnston ended up playing at the highest levels in Scotland and England and also starred for their country, while Locke lifted the Scottish Cup as Hearts captain in 1996 and also played in the English top flight. These boys set the benchmark of the quality we had and at that time I knew, with a bit of luck, we were on the verge of a real golden generation of up-and-coming talent.

The men responsible for bringing this special group together were the Hearts scouts Roy Tomnay and Douglas Dalgleish. Roy covered the Glasgow side while Douglas was responsible for Edinburgh and the east coast. Between them they brought hundreds of thousands of pounds worth of talent to Tynecastle. The jobs they did for the club should never be underestimated.

Allan Johnston was a protégé of Roy, and from a young age offered real quality on the ball. He had the ability to go out and win games on his own and that was part of the reason he earned his nickname 'Magic' after the American basketball legend Magic Johnson. I gave him a far less flattering nickname, however, when I labelled him 'Sticky' because when he first came into Hearts he was like a stick insect. He was one of the skinniest kids I have ever seen at a young age and he was also pretty weak but boy could he play. We continued to work hard on his fitness and physique, although when it came to whether or not he would break into the first team, that was still open to debate. I knew he had the talent, but I was still a bit unsure of whether he could cope with the physical demands and rigours of top-level football. Roy Tomnay knew Allan better than anybody and argued his case with me all the way. I was still concerned but decided to put my trust in Roy and gave Allan his chance. It is fair to say he didn't disappoint. His career never looked back and he went on to play for Scotland and carved out a fine career for himself with the French side Rennes before he returned to the UK to star for Sunderland, Middlesbrough and Rangers. It was funny that towards the end of his career Allan actually played in the same team as my youngest son, Nicky, in the First Division with Queen of the South.

Dougie Dalgleish was responsible for bringing in a Hearts-daft boy that went by the name of Gary Locke. I first came across Gary when he was a raw fourteen-year-old. He was a highly energetic midfielder who was combative in the challenge. He was a good footballer and quickly caught the eye. I felt he had a real chance but by the time he had turned sixteen he began to struggle physically because he was badly affected by growing pains. Gary was a wee bit gangly and his problems took a lot away from his game as he really struggled. I know from my own experience how serious growing pain can impact on you, especially if you are trying to make it as a professional foot-baller. It can affect your timing and cause you to lose your sharp-ness. Gary lost his way a wee bit but, to be fair to him, he never let his head go down and continued to battle on. I believed he was good enough and was determined to stick by him. I knew he could become a potential first-team player but there was a time when the club could have given up on him just after Alex MacDonald was replaced by Joe Jordan. Big Joe was trying to decide on his professional contracts for the following season so he watched all the trainees personally before he decided who should be signed and who was to be freed. If I am being honest Gary didn't show up well and really didn't impress. Joe, understandably, had his doubts but I told him not to worry about Gary. I explained the situation Gary had with the growing pains and I assured him he was a player in the making. To be fair to Joe he took my advice on board and signed Gary. He could quite easily have shown him the door but he was aware I knew Gary well and Joe trusted my judgement. I wonder how many young lads have been lost to the game in those sort of circumstances? If I had left Hearts with Alex MacDonald then Gary may never have been a Hearts player. Thankfully, I was proved right and Gary turned into a great player and loyal servant to Hearts. His obvious highlight was lifting the 1998 Scottish Cup as the Hearts captain under Jim Jefferies. Gary went on to play in England's top flight with Bradford City before he returned to Scotland to play for Kilmarnock. He was really unlucky with injury because he could have achieved an awful lot more, but he can look back on his career with great pride. Now Gary is in coaching and is passing his own experiences on to the next generation of stars; if he helps to uncover a few players as good as he was then he'll have done a decent job.

It was great working with the youngsters and it gave me a buzz and sense of fulfilment. The highlight, for me, was when my young Hearts team won the BP Youth Cup back in 1993. That was where some of our stars of the future, like Gary Locke and Paul Ritchie, really started to shine. We had a good team and squad, the captain Paul Weatherston, Myles Hogarth, David Murie, Grant Murray, Allan McManus, Colin Walker, Kevin Thomas, Mark Bradley, Stuart Callaghan, Gordon Connelly and Grant Duncan. We had a good solid base from which to build. We had Hogarth between the sticks and in front of them I usually went with three central defenders. They were normally Paul Ritchie, Allan McManus and Grant Murray who was the sweeper. Alan Rae, the legendary Hearts physiotherapist, who is a great football man and knows the game inside out, joked one day, 'You have two Alsatians there and if you are lucky enough to get past them then you have a Rottweiler [in Grant Murray] waiting behind them.' It was a great statement that summed up how strong we were defensively.

At either side of my dogged defence I had David Murie and Paul Weatherston pushing up either flank and we also had good players in the middle to front areas who could make things happen, like Gary Locke, Kevin Thomas and Stuart Callaghan. I felt we were as good as if not better than the other teams at our level and the team showed that on their glory BP Youth Cup run. We got to the final by beating Hamilton, Dundee, Kilmarnock, Ayr United and then Montrose in the semi-final, who we smashed pretty convincingly 7–0. Even when we made the final we were still seen as the underdogs because we were playing Rangers at Ibrox. That suited us because it just let us go and focus on our football. I knew if we played to our capabilities we would win games and that proved to be the case. We won 3–1 thanks to goals from Kevin Thomas, Alan McManus and David Murie and it would have been a bit more convincing had Stuart Callaghan not missed a penalty. It was a fantastic achievement for the boys, the team and the football club.

The one thing that did infuriate me that season was the lack of recognition our boys got on the Scotland front. We had shown we were one of the top teams but our players were continually overlooked at youth level. It was absolutely criminal because our players were as good as, if not better than, the other boys who were getting picked. It seemed if you played for Celtic or Rangers then you were guaranteed a call-up regardless of ability. It upset me and I made no secret of the fact. And I used it as part of my team talks, especially when we played Rangers or Celtic. I would tell the boys to go out and prove the people at the SFA wrong by showing they were better than the guys who were being picked ahead of them, which helped to motivate our players.

I knew all the boys from the BP Youth Cup-winning team weren't all going to make it at Tynecastle but I still felt a fair number of them would be able to make a name for themselves in the game, even if it meant dropping down the leagues. Paul Ritchie, Allan McManus, Gary Locke, Grant Murray and Kevin Thomas all made an impression in the Hearts first team, while the likes of Myles Hogarth, Stuart Callaghan, David Murie and Mark Bradley have all done well for themselves further down the leagues. There were a few who decided to choose careers away from football, like the skipper Paul Weatherston, but every one of those boys, who was part of that BP Youth Cup triumph, can look back and be extremely proud of their efforts. I am certainly proud of every single one of them.

We also managed to get to the Reserve League Cup final. The day of the game Wallace Mercer had been out for lunch and had had quite a few glasses of red wine. He came into the coach's room that afternoon and told us that he wanted to win the cup and was going to give our players £250 a man for a win. That bonus was similar to what the first-team players were on, so it was some incentive for the boys to do well. We played Dundee United in the final and there was no way we were going to lose. I remember John Clark played for Dundee United that day. He asked me what was going on because our boys had been so fired up. I told him what Wallace had offered and even he was shocked because, as I said, it was a lot of money back then. We won the game pretty convincingly and the players walked off the pitch a heck of a lot better off.

We won the reserve league, too, as we pipped Dundee United to the title and managed to get there without kicking a ball.

Dundee United went to Falkirk and needed to win but they lost and so we were crowned champions. It was good to win the league but when managing the Hearts reserve team winning games wasn't the be all and end all; obviously, you wanted to win as many games as you could but it was more about developing young players and getting them ready for the first team. The good thing about the Tynecastle board, mainly Pilmar Smith and Les Porteous, was that they were really supportive of the youth set-up and recognised how important it was to the club. The other big thing was that reserve games were used to give out-of-favour players or guys who were coming back from injury a chance to top up their fitness. Reserve football was really beneficial and, as far as I am concerned, it is badly missed in the Scottish Premier League today. There must be some way, even under the current financial constraints, of resurrecting the reserve league.

I know not all young players are going to make it, there are always going to be casualties along the way. Even those who are tipped for greatness can fall short of what is required, as was the case with young Tommy Harrison. He was the young star player in the Hearts set-up, when I first started coaching, who was predicted to become the Darren Fletcher of his time. The club really had high hopes for him and thought he was going to be their next superstar. Manchester United and a host of big English clubs all tried to sign him but Wallace Mercer pushed the boat out to make sure he came to Tynecastle. Wallace ended up giving him a lot of money, I think it was about £40,000, just so he would sign on as a schoolboy with Hearts. I have to say that I didn't share the same enthusiasm as the masses, who claimed Tommy was going to be the next big thing. Yes, he was a decent player but I wasn't really sure if he was going to hit the heights everybody was predicting. I played with him early on in a reserve game at Meadowbank. I thought he had a quiet game and began to doubt my own judgement because I was just starting out on my coaching career. In the end, Tommy never made it because of a bad injury that all but ended his hopes of making a name for himself. That must have been a real hammer blow to take. It is a disappointment when boys fail to make the grade but, unfortunately, that is part and parcel of professional football, not everyone is going is going to make the grade. I think during my time at Tynecastle we had more than our fair share of success in bringing young players through and it certainly flew in the face of criticism that said the club didn't have any decent young players coming through.

18

MY MANAGERIAL DEBT TO HEARTS

HEARTS FINISHED second under Joe Jordan's stewardship in the 1991–92 season but struggled to hit such heights again. Joe was sacked at the end of the 1992–93 season as we struggled and he left with three games to go. Wallace Mercer appointed me as caretaker manager and in the end, we finished fifth in the league and qualified for the UEFA Cup. I was invited out to see Wallace in the south of France at the end of the season. Wallace was based out there for tax reasons and would only come back to Scotland now and again. I flew out with the vice chairman Pilmar Smith to discuss the plans for the new season. Wallace had already told me on the phone before I flew out that I was getting the manager's job on a permanent basis – it was only a case of dotting the i's and crossing the t's – so when I got out there we quickly agreed my contract and I signed a two-year deal.

I was delighted to get the chance to manage a club that meant so much to me. I felt ready to manage a top team and I was determined to do well. I had learned from my experience at Partick Thistle and I was confident I could do a good job at Tynecastle. I had also been coaching and learning my trade under some top managers like Alex MacDonald, Sandy Jardine and Joe Jordan. I always wanted to return to management and if I could have picked any job then it would have been Hearts. I had some great times there as a player and I had such a strong bond with the fans. I just wanted to reward them with some success and to build the team back up again

I then set about looking for an assistant manager. Initially, I tried to get Billy Kirkwood from Rangers, I spoke to Walter Smith, who was the Ibrox manager, but he didn't want to let him go. Walter told me no, but would leave the final decision up to Billy, but Billy decided to stay at Rangers and I would have to wait a few years before that partnership was to come to fruition. I turned my attentions to Hugh McCann. I had done my SFA A Licence with Hugh and I wanted to bring somebody in that didn't really know me, I didn't want somebody who would be a nodding dog and agree with everything I said. I wanted my assistant to have an input and I felt Hugh would do that, he also had managerial experience, albeit at a lower level with Alloa Athletic. Hugh and I hit it off right away, we built up a close bond and worked well together.

Wallace was also in the process of trying to sell the club and was looking to cut the debt to make Hearts look like a more attractive proposition to potential buyers. There was also the cost of meeting the Taylor Report and making Tynecastle an all-seated stadium, so it was far to say that spending money on the first team wasn't exactly Wallace's priority. My initial remit was to drastically reduce the wage bill and the overdraft by £1 million. It was a transitional period for the club and I knew it was going to be a difficult season in a lot of ways.

The only way I was going to be able to hit the chairman's savings was to play the young players that I had developed from the youths up into the reserves. They were the one shining light for me because I knew the likes of Gary Locke, Allan McManus, Paul Ritchie, Allan Johnston and Kevin Thomas were all good enough to make a name for themselves at Hearts. They had just lifted the under-19 BP Cup and needed the chance and somebody to show faith in them. Joe Jordan could have played some of them earlier but he didn't. I totally understood why he didn't take the risk because he was looking for his team to challenge for the title and also had a bigger budget and a lot of experienced players. Joe had strength and depth in his squad and felt his teams could challenge for the title but the one thing I would say about Joe is that he was always supportive of the youth set-up and the young players during his time at Hearts.

I was quite relaxed about the situation because I had faith in the young players who were at the club and I knew that given time they could become real assets. In the meantime, I had to bring some money in and that meant selling one of my main players. I ended up selling Derek Ferguson to Sunderland, where Terry Butcher was the manager, for £500,000 and got John Colquhoun back in exchange. Derek was a great player but the club needed money and I had very little choice. I knew John, having played with him, and I was certain he would do a good job for us on his return, and the money from the sale of Derek helped clear a large chunk of the club's overdraft. I also managed to move quite a few other big-earners on and reduced the wage bill significantly. Joe had taken in quite a lot of players on decent money but I managed to shift guys like Ian Baird, Glynn Snodin, Peter Van De Ven and Gary Williams on.

I still had to strengthen my squad although funds were limited. I needed a replacement for Ian Baird and signed Justin Fashanu, who I will tell you a bit more about later, and Jim Weir from Hamilton. Jim was a good, solid and commanding centre half. I rushed that deal through to get him on board for the European games with Atletico Madrid in the UEFA Cup. We paid quite a bit of money for Jim but for one reason or another it didn't really happen for him at Hearts, although he still went on to have a decent playing career and is now doing well in management. It was a bit of a shame because I believed Jim would be a real asset to the team as he had all the physical attributes needed to be a top central defender. He also had a great attitude into the bargain but maybe Hearts were just too big a club for him at that time. Apart from those additions I pretty much had to go with what I had inherited. The good thing was I still had a core of good experienced players. My captain was Craig Levein, who did really well for me, and there was my former strike partner John Robertson, Gary Mackay and Neil Berry, who I had played along-side. There was also Alan McLaren, who was another promising young defender, so I had the basis of a decent squad.

We lost the first game of the season away at Ibrox but after that we went on a good run and climbed as high as second in the table. We also won 1–0 over Hibs. Allan Johnston scored the only goal of the game and it really was a terrific strike. He fired a right foot volley high into the top corner. I was delighted for the fans because I know how important this fixture is to them and it was also special for me although even bigger for Allan. I had seen him grow as a player and a person and here he was starring for Hearts. That win over Hibs was a real high but I knew the team were still finding their feet and there were going to be plenty more ups and downs.

We drew Atletico Madrid in the UEFA Cup. The first game was at Tynecastle and it was a real typical Scottish night. It was damp and wet for the first leg at Tynecastle and it obviously put off the Swedish referee Bo Karlsson. He called off before kickoff and was replaced by his fellow countryman Anders Frisk, who went on to make a name for himself as a top-flight referee. Atletico were a good team but they also adopted a typical European approach. Their players would go down under the slightest contact and roll about like they had been shot, it was frustrating but part and parcel. The good thing for me was that despite Atletico's quality we more than matched them on the night. The Hearts fans were a twelfth man and really had Tynecastle rocking that night. We went in goal-less at half-time and then with twenty minutes to go we shocked the Spaniards. Gary Locke, who was superb in the game, curled in a free kick that Justin Fashanu got his head on but their goalkeeper, Diego, managed to get a hand on it, before it fell to John Robertson inside the six-yard box. He didn't need a second invitation to stick it away. We were suddenly 1–0 up and I was standing on the touchline pinching myself but things got even better five minutes later when we doubled our lead. Locke was the creator again when he released John Colquhoun, who took it down and coolly stuck the ball away. It was a real great European performance and I thought if we can hold on to this lead then we would have a great chance going out to Madrid for the second leg. It wasn't to be because Atletico's Polish striker Roman Kosecki came off the bench to score a solo effort to put a bit of a dampener on what was still a great European night for Hearts. That away goal, however, gave Atletico hope and we knew we would be up against it in the Vicente Calderon Stadium – which is one of the real hotbeds of Spanish football.

Our European preparations were at least aided as we beat Celtic at Tynecastle. John Robertson scored the only goal of the game and helped boost the confidence but I knew it was still going to be a big ask heading out to Spain. It proved to be the case as Atletico showed their class and put us to the sword. They thumped us 3–0 to end our European adventure. It was no disgrace to bow out to a team of Atletico's class. Maybe things might have been different had we not lost that away goal but I was still proud of the performances my players put on over those two games. We gave it our best shot, although in the end it just wasn't quite good enough.

Our bread and butter was always going to be the league and John Robertson conjured up more derby magic to lift our European hangover. He scored twice as we beat Hibs at Easter Road. 'Wee Robbo' really was the hammer of Hibs when you look at his record. My record against Hibs was good but John's is even better, it was absolutely phenomenal. John was in his second spell at the club after he returned from Newcastle. It took him a wee while to find his feet again because his confidence had taken a bit of a dent after his time at St James Park. There is no question he played his best football in the maroon of Hearts and even in that season he finished our top scorer and netted some important goals for the team.

Just before that Easter Road game I still felt we were a bit short of striking options. We had John but Justin Fashanu started to struggle with his on-going knee problem so we needed a bit more competition. I had heard that Maurice Johnston was looking to leave Everton and would consider a return to Scotland. I managed to convince Wallace to make more money available to put a package together that would give us a chance of landing Mo, and I arranged a meeting. Mo had played at the highest level with Scotland, Celtic, Rangers and Everton but when I met him what struck me about him was his enthusiasm and his desire to play. He wanted to come to Hearts and quickly agreed a deal. The good thing for us, just as well, was that it wasn't about the money for Mo, he had made his money out of football and wanted the chance to show he could still play at the highest level. I knew what he was like as a player and his attitude from day one was spot on. Some people might view Mo as a bit of a 'Flash Harry' but he is one of the hardest-working professionals I have come across. I remember one training session when the boys started moaning about what we were doing. I ended up losing the plot, put the balls away and made them run for the rest of the session. Mo moaned non-stop but, to be fair to him, he led the running from start to finish. He was a good professional and someone the younger players could look up to and learn from. He might have lived life to the full but he also gave his football 100 percent.

I had a lot of good players but it was a difficult time for the club. It was a steep learning curve; it was hard but I think a lot of experienced managers would also have struggled working in the circumstances I found myself in, with everything that was going on behind the scenes, from the rebuilding of Tynecastle to the club being up for sale. I remember speaking to Alex MacDonald and he told me that football management can be the loneliest job in the world because when it comes to the crunch the buck stops with you. You can employ as many people as you like but you have to stand or fall by the decisions you make, your signings, tactics and the teams you pick. It was a difficult, difficult year, although it was also enjoyable, knowing I was manager of Hearts. The thing that never left me was my self-belief. I never had any doubts I could do the job. I knew the squad would get better and the younger players would kick on with every game they played.

19

JUSTIN FASHANU AND HIS
TABLOID TALES

I FELT we needed more of a physical presence up front, somebody who could hold the ball up and really be a decent foil for John Robertson. Ian Baird went to Bristol City with the fee being decided by a tribunal. We got good money and ended up receiving around £300,000 for Ian. I started to cast my eye around for possible alternatives but the problem was that we weren't exactly awash with cash. Money was tight and I needed to get the best I could from the limited resources I had available.

Justin Fashanu was a player I immediately thought could be our man. He had been at Airdrie under my former boss, Alex MacDonald, and had done really well for them in the Scottish top flight. My old team had struggled and got relegated but Fashanu had still been one of their top performers. I spoke to Alex and he told me that Justin would definitely do Hearts a turn. I also had Walter Kidd on my coaching staff at Hearts and he had played alongside him with Airdrie and couldn't have spoken more highly about Justin as a player or a person.

Justin had an impressive playing CV. He had been a million-pound player and had starred for some top clubs like Norwich City, Nottingham Forest, Notts County, Manchester City and West Ham United. The problem was Justin had a bad knee and couldn't train all the time. I knew that but felt if we could manage his training then he could be a real asset to the team. Justin had also kept himself fit after he had left Airdrie by having a short spell with the Swedish side Trelleborg.

I knew that Justin would fall into our budget. If he had been fully-fit then we would have had no chance of bringing him to Hearts because he would have still been in the English top flight. The good thing for us was that Justin had been at Airdrie and had really enjoyed his time in Scotland, that worked in our favour and Justin also viewed Hearts as a step up. He was being given the chance to play for a big-city club and I think that also appealed to him because he was quite a flamboyant character. He was also a real charmer. People always spoke about Justin's sexuality. It was well known that he was homo-sexual, but to be fair to Justin, the ladies loved him as well. He was a big, handsome guy and would have people eating out of his hands, a real gentleman and a pretty articulate guy into the bargain.

A lot was made of Justin's sexuality throughout his career but for me and everybody else at Hearts it was all about Justin Fashanu the footballer. One of the red-top tabloid newspapers rather cruelly dubbed Justin 'The Queen of Hearts' but that was a cheap dig. It didn't matter to the fans, the players or anybody connected to the club. Justin, to be fair, was proud of his sexu-ality and was an icon to a lot of people in the game and in everyday life. The big man was also good to have in the Tynecastle dressing room.

The only wee laugh I had about Justin's signing was via John Robertson. We went on a pre-season tour to Germany and I decided to room Justin with the wee man. Wee Robbo now tells the story of that first night in the hotel room when he is doing his after-dinner speaking. He joked that he never slept a wink and when he looked round all he could see was Justin's big white eyes staring at him. I don't know why John was so worried – it was clear that Justin had a lot better taste!

Justin made his debut against Rangers and immediately showed the quality he had. He scored his only goal for us against Partick Thistle, but unfortunately because of the knee injury we never saw him often enough. Justin didn't play a lot of games, but when he did take to the field he still made a half-decent impact.

Away from Tynecastle, Justin was making a name for himself in Edinburgh. I know he had some wild parties and there was a lot of stuff going on, but I didn't want anything to do with it. I was his manager and as long as he was training when he was told and playing on a Saturday then I left him to his own devices. He lived in the New Town and became a bit of a socialite – he was friendly with celebrities, government officials and some of the city's most successful businessmen. There were even stories, at one point, that he was going to buy the City Cafe bar in Blair Street. He just loved the buzz of capital life.

To be fair to Justin there was never any show without punch. He had been friendly with Julie Goodyear, who had played Bet Lynch in *Coronation Street*, and he loved to see his name in the papers. He once said to me that there was no such thing as bad publicity. He loved the limelight and being the centre of attention. His view was that any press coverage, good or bad, had to be good for his profile. It didn't matter to him if he was making the back pages for scoring a hat-trick or the front pages for his off-the-field antics. Anything that got him in the papers then Justin was happy to help, whether it be with a few quotes or a photograph. He was certainly media-friendly and saw it as a way of raising his profile and of making extra cash. He wanted to make as much money as he could knowing that his career was on the way down.

It was that desire to get his name into the headlines that eventually led to his downfall with Hearts. Justin went to the *News of the World* and then *The People* to try and sell a story that he had slept with two male MPs. He demanded a six-figure sum for his story but, in the end, neither paper decided to run it. It then came out that Justin had tried to sell his story. He initially denied the claims but eventually realised he had got himself in too deep and had to hold his hands up and admit he had lied.

Right away the chairman, Wallace Mercer, the board and I all agreed that we could no longer keep Justin at the club. That was him finished and there was no turning back. He had crossed the line and his actions had been a step too far. There was only going to be one conclusion and that was to terminate his contract. He had breached his contract by his actions and left us with no option but to show him the door. The story in itself was bad enough but I was more disappointed that Justin hadn't come to me and let me know or warned somebody at the club about what was going to come out. There were clearly other things going on behind the scenes that Justin had failed to tell us. There had always been stories and rumours surrounding Justin and his private life but I never took too much notice of it because most of it was mostly gossip.

As soon as the newspapers ran the story that Justin had tried to sell his story he just disappeared and we never saw him again. Justin was never seen back at the club again and never came back to pick up his boots or any of his gear. I tried to get a hold of him and phoned all the numbers I had for him but it was all in vain. He fled his Edinburgh flat and was never seen in the city again. He disappeared off the radar before he eventually pitched up in America a few months later. There were all sorts of stories going around including further allegations that he had been involved in a very heavy situation that had led to his life being threatened and that was why he decided to flee. There were also claims that there was a government cover-up but the real circumstances have never been uncovered and we were left with more questions than answers. It must have been pretty serious but nobody apart from Justin and a few others really knew what actually went on.

When you look at Justin's life he went through some difficult times, from being raised in a home by Barnardo's right to the way it all ended for him. There are stories that his brother, the former England international John Fashanu, had disowned him. I don't know if that was right or not, but it was certainly a tragedy that he ended up taking his own life. It was a great shame because, as a person, I really liked Justin. I enjoyed working with him and he was a big, decent guy. Justin always lived life on the edge and he had obviously gone as far as he thought he could.

Looking back, I have no regrets about signing Justin. I would still have signed him even though it didn't work out as well as either of us had hoped. That was more down to injury than anything else because when he was fit he was a top-class player and a good person.

20

THE GREAT ESCAPE

THE SECOND half of the 1993–94 season was always going to be a fraught affair. The Scottish Premier Division was about to be revamped again. From the start of the following season it was going to be cut from twelve teams down to ten, which meant three teams were going to take the dreaded drop into the First Division. Relegation was a financial nightmare to every top-flight club although it would probably have impacted Hearts a lot more than it would have some others, due to the financial situation we were in. Around the Christmas period we had toiled and were sitting in ninth place, just one above the relegation slots.

There was a bit of concern but I had faith in the players and in my own abilities. Still I also knew that things at the bottom end of the table were really tight. I had the full backing of Wallace Mercer, although little did I know that not all of his fellow directors had the same faith in me. Jim Clydesdale had gone behind my back to Wallace and told him that I was struggling and thought the job of being Hearts manager was too big for me. The disappointing thing was that Jim never said anything to my face. When Wallace ended up coming back from France and told me he wanted to meet up, I didn't think it was anything out of the ordinary because we normally got together whenever Wallace came back.

The meeting went along the usual lines of, how are you getting on and how are things? I gave him my thoughts and views and told him where we should be looking to make improvements. We had a good chat and Wallace accepted everything I had said and then admitted he was more than happy with the job I was doing. I didn't think any more about it but then about a month later Wallace said to me, 'Do you know why we had that meeting? Jim Clydesdale had said to me that he thought you were struggling in the job. I came back to see for myself. I thought you were alright, I just wanted to look into your eyes to see you were okay. When I did that I was fine.' I wasn't exactly too pleased with Mr Clydesdale when I heard that, although I was reassured to know that I still had the full backing of the chairman.

The fans realised the club was in a transitional period and to their credit they stuck by me and the team. That was something I really appreciated because they could quite easily have turned against us but they knew, together, we could get Hearts back on a far stronger footing by being united. I think I also got a bit of extra leeway because I was a former Hearts player and I went that season unbeaten against Hibs. I am sure that helped me a lot. The New Year game at Tynecastle was a big result although one of my own players, unknown to him, had turned into an unlikely informer for our Edinburgh rivals.

We stayed the night before a game at The Marine Hotel in North Berwick, which I used quite a lot for our pre-match preparations. It had been a popular haunt from when Alex MacDonald had been the manager. I was at the hotel with the team the night before the game. We trained in the afternoon and then I named my team after it, to give the players a chance to prepare. That evening I took a call from Les Porteous, the club secretary. He said, 'Have you picked your team? And is it Smith . . . ?', and he rhymed off my team from one to eleven. I said, 'How do you know that?' He told me it was out and Hibs had got a hold of it. I was raging, but, if I am being honest, I never thought once about changing my team just because Hibs knew who was playing. I still felt that was my strongest team and I had faith they would get us a result. My biggest concern wasn't Hibs but how the team had actually leaked out. I just couldn't believe it because the only people who knew who was starting were the players, the coaching staff and me. It was a time before mobile phones so I went to the front reception desk and asked the receptionist to check all the calls made from all our rooms. I didn't think for one second that one of our own was going to deliberately put the team out into the public domain but I just needed to check. I was delighted when the call records came back and there was nothing untoward with any of the calls. I eventually found out after the game what had happened. Gary Locke had phoned his dad and told him he was starting and told him the rest of the team. Mr Locke senior then went to the pub, had a few drinks, and told all his mates what the team was, and that was how it had come out. I have to say, if I was looking for a culprit then Mr Locke senior would have been one of the last people I would have suspected. You would struggle to find a bigger Hearts fan than him. The entire family are Jambos through and through and love to see the team get one over the Hibees. Thankfully, it didn't affect us too much because, as I said, we still managed to get a point in a 1–1 draw through a magnificent goal from John Millar. To be fair, John did well for me and deserves a lot of credit for his performances that season because I have to say, at first I didn't really fancy him too much. If I had had the chance I would have moved him on. I don't know if John sensed that or not but he just got on with things, kept his head down, worked hard and when he got his chance he never let me or the team down. John ended up being one of the first names on my team sheet.

The results against Hibs were fine but we also had to raise our game against our fellow relegation rivals. There wasn't much between the teams at all, outside Rangers. Teams didn't have the same financial clout as they have even today. The highest earners at the club were John Robertson and Craig Levein and they were both on £1,000 a week. They were at the very top end and there weren't too many round about them in that higher bracket.

The turn of the year saw us spark into life. We lost only four games during that second period and in normal circumstances that sort of form would have seen us pushing for a European place. The problem was that all the other teams were also picking up points. Knowing the fear of relegation was looming for at least a quarter of the Premier Division, it turned out to be a real dogfight. Credit to the likes of St Johnstone and Thistle because they kept picking up points and we were never able to pull away.

Around that time, I signed Stevie Frail from Dundee. 'Shaggy', as he is known, came in at the start of April and played the last eight or nine games of the season. He was a really good signing for the club a solid and reliable full back, who had good energy and could get up and down the park. He was a big player in those closing games.

It came down to the final game of the season against Partick Thistle. It was rather ironic that after my spell at Firhill that I could have ended relegating them but in all honesty it didn't really enter my thoughts. My one and only concern was making sure that Hearts stayed up. It was a mammoth game and there was a lot of pressure on us, Hearts are a massive club and it would have been a disaster if we had ended up being relegated. I have to say I went into that match confident that we would get the result we needed. We had been playing well, the spirit amongst the boys was high and everybody at the club had a real togetherness and desire to make sure we didn't end up in trouble. I certainly knew we were good enough and we also had great backing from the Hearts support who really rallied in the final weeks of that season. We took a big travelling support through to Firhill, with the club putting on free buses to try and aid our survival fight, for that final day. It was a pretty poor and nervous game but we never looked in any real danger, even though we lost big Jim Weir with a nasty face knock. We managed to keep things tight and three minutes from time we got the goal that secured our top flight survival when Alan McLaren headed a John Robertson corner into the net. I knew at that point we were going to be safe but there was a fair amount of fear around the home sections at Firhill. St Johnstone were in the relegation zone and were beating Motherwell. If Saints or ourselves had scored another goal then John Lambie's Thistle would have gone down. Mo Johnston, who had started out at Firhill, had a late chance but he missed and Thistle survived along with ourselves. In the end, it was St Johnstone, Raith Rovers and Dundee who took the drop. Ironically, our final day win actually took us up to joint sixth so that showed how tight things were in the bottom half. It was just a huge relief to know we were safe and in the end, I think we deserved to stay up. We only lost one game, to Dundee, in our final ten games and so, all in all, that wasn't a bad way to sign off the season.

After that, we headed to Canada for a pre-season tour and my thoughts immediately went to how I could take the team on. We had good players but I still felt we needed a wee bit more quality. I knew if we could start the next season the way we had finished the second half of the previous campaign then we could have been on the verge of achieving something really special – or so I thought!

21

THE PIEMAN AND ALL HIS MINCE

THERE HAD been a lot of speculation in the newspapers and press that a catering tycoon called Chris Robinson had been trying to raise the funds to buy Hearts from Wallace Mercer. Robinson had made his name and his money through Wheatsheaf Catering. They did a lot of their business with football clubs, providing food and drinks at the kiosks around a lot of the grounds in Scotland. That was how he got his nickname 'The Pieman'. I didn't know much about him personally and, in all honesty, it wasn't really my concern, I was just focused on trying to strengthen our first team. I knew I had to put all the speculation about the club's future to one side. If I didn't then I wouldn't have been professional and I wouldn't have been operating in the best interests of Hearts. I continued to give things my all and if the takeover happened it happened. I would deal with it when and if I had to. I knew any new owner might want to bring in their own manager, I accepted that but at the same time I couldn't sit about worrying about things. There was a job to do and Hearts were too big a club to simply stand still – despite the financial constraints I had been forced to operate under.

That pre-season we were invited to Canada for a summer tournament along with our Scottish rivals Celtic and Aberdeen. We all travelled out and played in this tournament in Toronto. Pilmar

Smith, our vice chairman, came out with us as part of the official party because Wallace had stayed back in Scotland. Pilmar was a great guy, a real Hearts man and was always very supportive of me. After our final game out in Canada, Pilmar came up to me and told me that the chairman had been on the phone. Wallace had told him that we had to go right away and get our £10,000 appearance money from the sponsor and put it straight into the club's bank account. This was a bit strange, to say the least, because it wasn't exactly a massive fortune. I agreed to go with Pilmar to get our money. We got it, cashed it and never thought too much about it. We went to the sponsors and then had to go to their bank to get the money wired back to Scotland. It all seemed a bit bizarre but we knew Wallace and there would be method behind his madness, we just didn't know, at that point, what he was up to. Things were to became clearer a few days later.

We came back from Canada when Wallace pulled me to one side and told me he had agreed a deal to sell the club to Robinson. It quickly became clear that Wallace had wanted all the money that had been due, including our appearance money from Canada, so he could improve the club's balance sheet, knowing he would get even more money when he sold his majority share-holding. He had put the money in and drove the club, so nobody could really argue with what he had done.

I still remember the conversation when he broke the news to me that Friday afternoon. He told me that he had agreed to sell to Robinson and Leslie Deans, and then Wallace added, 'I wouldn't worry about things because I spoke to Chris Robinson and he really likes you.' I thought to myself right away that is me on the way out. I had a gut feeling that Robinson didn't fancy me, despite what my departing chairman had told me. I knew Wallace didn't really know what Robinson's plans were and probably wasn't even bothered. He was getting his money and he was getting out, and that was all that concerned him.

The one thing I have to be thankful to Wallace for was that he gave me that initial two-year contract and it still had another twelve months left to run. The sale of the club was finalised the next day and Wallace celebrated by flying off to America on Concorde that weekend. Come the Monday I was checking out of Tynecastle, having been sacked as Hearts manager.

Robinson and Deans had come into the club for the first time. Ironically, it was also a big day for the club for other reasons. That same afternoon the central beam of the new Wheatfield Stand was put in place and the club had organised a bit of a celebratory party to mark the occasion. A lot of figureheads from the council and city dignitaries were all invited to a bit of a party at the club. Knowing Wallace, he probably arranged the party before he jetted off.

Financially, the club may have been struggling under Wallace but he should be given a lot of credit for what he did for Hearts. He played a huge part in redeveloping Tynecastle.

I still didn't know what was happening that Monday when Robinson and Deans came into the club. They bought over the club together but it was Robinson who called most of the shots. Hugh McCann, my assistant manager, and I went into Tynecastle, determined to carry on our jobs as normal or until we were told otherwise. That day there were all these people milling around the Tynecastle boardroom, drinking wine and eating nibbles. I remember I left proceedings and went out into the stadium. I sat and watched the workmen continue their work on the Wheatfield Stand. Everything was going round my head and I thought to myself, 'I can't let this go on. I need to find out where I stand'. I got hold of Hugh and he agreed with me. We went and grabbed Chris and Leslie in the boardroom and asked if we could speak to them. I then asked, 'What is happening?' Robinson's reply was simple although crushing. He said, 'I am sacking you.' I didn't wait for an explanation and in total disgust I stood up, shook my head and walked out, slamming the door behind me. I was reeling and it hurt, but he had made his decision and nothing I was going to say or do was going to change his mind. It wasn't a total shock but it was still hard to take. I had been at Hearts for ten years and felt I had done a lot of good work in my first season as manager and I knew I was really getting somewhere with the club. We had brought through some good young players, had come through a difficult season, had reduced the debt and put the club in a far healthier position than it had been in previous years. Now I was being binned and somebody was going to reap the rewards of all my hard work. It was a sad day when I walked out of Tynecastle with my bag of belongings for that final time. I loved my time at Hearts and I still love going back to Tynecastle to watch games but that was a sad, sad day. Thankfully, we had John Millar's wedding that same night and that helped ease some of my pain, even if it was only a temporary measure. Quite a few of the players were there that night and it gave me a chance to say my thank yous and goodbyes.

It was disappointing but it was Robinson's prerogative to hire or fire who he wanted. He had put his money up and was entitled to call the shots the way he saw them. I could accept that, but the thing that really angered me was the way he made me fight tooth and nail to get my contract paid up. The club had stopped Hugh's and my wages the same day we were sacked. Previous Hearts managers, after they had left the club, had received their wages three or four weeks after they had departed. I said to Hugh when we got sacked, 'Don't worry, we will still get three or four weeks' wages because that is the way the club works.'

How wrong I was. Our wages were stopped with immediate effect and Hugh and I were left without a bean and worrying about where our next wage packet was going to come from.

Robinson, initially, made no attempt to pay us the money we were due. I eventually had to go to a lawyer, Ian Corbett, who I had previously used. We had to threaten court action before Robinson and the club finally settled my contract which took a fair amount of time. If this hadn't dragged on for so long then we could all have drawn a line under things and moved on. I don't know if he had been struggling to find the money to pay up our contracts or just didn't want to pay us. Maybe he had stretched himself to the limit and thought we could wait a wee bit longer for our money. What annoyed me was the fact he didn't give me, Hugh or our families a second thought. He showed no interest and for all he knew we could have been out on the street – that was what really annoyed me.

I never saw Robinson again until I went to a Celtic game to do a bit of scouting for Alex McLeish at Motherwell. Celtic played at Hampden for a season while they redeveloped Celtic Park. Wheatsheaf were doing the catering at the national stadium. I went to the match with two of my mates, Gary Brown and Archie Meikle. I saw Robinson walking past me and I shouted at him. He turned and asked, 'How are you doing?' I absolutely lost it. I called him everything under the sun. He got both barrels. My two mates couldn't believe it, they stood there absolutely stunned and open-mouthed at the way I had reacted. They were street-wise guys but had never seen me act like that before, I probably never have and hopefully never will again. Looking back now it was a bit embarrassing but it made me feel an awful lot better, the fact I had got months and months of frustration and anger off my chest. I will always remember his response until the day I die. He just shrugged his shoulders and said, 'Sandy, I didn't do you any harm. I just sacked you.' At that point, I could have swung for him and if my mates hadn't been there then I think I probably would have lost it all together. There were a few times, after I was sacked, where I could have swung at him. We didn't have any money problems but we were forced to really tighten our belts. It wasn't as if I had earned the big money that players in the English Premier League pick up today, money was tight and there were a few low points and that was when the anger really festered. It was just down to the unfairness of it all.

By the point of that Hampden Park meeting, I had also learned a few things that had rubbed further salt into my wounds with regards my successor. The Motherwell manager and my old Rangers No. 2 Tommy McLean was the man Robinson had picked to replace me. It is funny how, with hindsight, you can look back on things differently. Tommy was both manager and director at Motherwell, and towards the end of my final season at Hearts he stepped down as a director and then eventually resigned as manager. It took a bit of time before he was finally named as my replacement at Hearts. I later heard stories that around the Christmas before I left Tommy had allegedly agreed with Robinson that he would become Hearts manager if Robinson got the club. These things happen in football, I certainly don't blame Tommy for taking the Hearts job because it is a great job, but I do blame him for not telling me if he did know what was happening. He had been the assistant manager when I played at Rangers and I got on well with him and respected him as an individual. Personally, I think I deserved more respect than I got from him during that whole sorry episode.

The irony of it all is that this must have been going on in the background at a time when I had got Hearts on a decent run. Even if Robinson had wanted to keep me as manager he had probably already committed to Tommy. He had no choice but to sack me.

If I had stayed at the club then the young players would have formed the nucleus of my Hearts team. My successor, Tommy McLean, didn't get the best out of them but his eventual replacement, Jim Jefferies, certainly did. He deserves enormous credit for developing that squad and adding to it further down the line.

They say in life that what goes around comes around. A few years later, when I was manager of St Johnstone, Robinson tried to get me to return to manage Hearts again. It was after Jim Jefferies left for Bradford City in 2000. My St Johnstone chairman, Geoff Brown, came into my office and said, 'Here is Chris Robinson's number. He wants to speak to you.' I said something along the lines of, 'Oh, really.' There had been a bit of speculation about it in the press but I had never really given it much notice. I took the piece of paper off Geoff and told him that I would give Robinson a call. Geoff said he didn't want to stand in my way, he knew my affiliation and feelings towards Hearts and would understand if I wanted to take the job again. I mulled things over for a couple of days and discussed things at length with my family before I went back to Geoff and said, 'I am not going to Hearts. I am not even interested in speaking to him.' I knew myself that it would have been impossible for me to work with Robinson. He had caused me and my family so much pain and hurt, I just couldn't have worked with him. It just wasn't the right thing for me to do. If somebody else had been in charge of Hearts then I would probably have gone back in a split-second. Too much water had gone under the bridge. I also don't think I will ever be able to forgive Robinson for the way he showed me the door.

They say every cloud has a silver lining and he eventually turned to another of my former Hearts teammates, Craig Levein. He had just started out in management at Cowdenbeath. I have to say I don't regret the decision I made. It was the right one for me – I am in no doubt about that.

I also have to say I took a lot of enjoyment going back to Tynecastle with other teams and getting one over on Mr Robinson's Hearts. For me, he was a poor ambassador for my former club. His time was hardly a success with all the financial problems and the turmoil before he eventually sold out to Vladimir Romanov. The fact he wanted to sell the ground to clear the debt just sums things up for me. Tynecastle means so much to so many people and selling that, to me, would be like cashing in on the family silver. It would have been unforgivable.

22

MANY HAPPY RETURNS AT HAMILTON ACCIES

I HAD been out of the game for a few months and the first phone call I took offering me a job came from Motherwell. Their assistant manager, Andy Watson, was somebody I knew well and had played alongside at Hearts. I also knew their manager, Alex McLeish. I had played against him a number of times and we always had a healthy respect for one another, unlike his Aberdeen central defensive partner Willie Miller. I had spoken to Alex at length that summer because he had been out in Toronto for the same pre-season tournament as Hearts. At that time he was still the Aberdeen captain and I was still Hearts boss. In a bizarre twist of fate, he was appointed as the player-manager of Motherwell, taking over from Tommy McLean who had replaced me at Hearts. Andy called me up and said, 'I don't want to embarrass you by offering you a job you maybe wouldn't want, but would you be interested in doing some part-time work for us, taking our reserve team and doing a bit of scouting for us?' I was out of football and was just pleased that Alex and Andy had thought I could bring something to Motherwell. I was delighted to get out and be involved in top-flight football again. I really enjoyed my time at Fir Park and I stayed there for a few months before I got the chance to cross the great Lanarkshire divide.

I had kept in touch with Iain Munro since we did our SFA coaching courses together and I played for him at Dunfermline. Iain had moved on and was the manager of Hamilton Accies. They were in the First Division when a vacancy came up for a community coach after Phil Bonnyman had moved on for a job in England, and that left Accies looking for a replacement. Iain put my name forward to the chief executive of the club, Alistair Duguid, so I met Alistair and those talks went well. It turned out that they wanted to change the role a bit. They asked me to work as the club's commercial manager and also as assistant to Iain Munro. I agreed to take the job because it was back in the game full-time and I knew I could benefit from working under Iain. I had worked with Iain at close quarters and I knew he was a top coach who I could learn from.

The chairman of Accies was David Campbell. He was a self-made millionaire thanks to the building trade. David had always been a Rangers fan but was encouraged to buy into the club by Duguid, who was a big Hamilton fan and one of his neighbours in Strathaven. Alastair and David were both first class to work for and we also had a good few nights out together. Davie had a lot of contacts from his businesses and that allowed me to open doors for both me and the club on the commercial side, which was important because it is fair to say Hamilton Accies, at that time, were not in the best of financial situations. They had sold their Douglas Park ground and had turned into the nomads of Scottish football. They played their home games at Partick Thistle's Firhill before they moved over to the home of our Lanarkshire rivals, Albion Rovers, at Cliftonhill. It was hard because there is no doubt the club lost a lot of its fan base by moving to Glasgow then Coatbridge. I suppose it was a case of needs must but it certainly didn't help.

That first year we finished sixth in the First Division but we struggled badly the following season and got relegated. We finished ninth but Iain Munro remained a man in demand. He initially went to St Mirren before he walked out on them for Raith Rovers. That 1995–96 season was a real hard one for the club. We had some decent players like the goalkeeper Allan Ferguson, Gary Clark and Martin McIntosh and we also had a young future Scotland star, Paul Hartley, in our ranks. Paul was a talented winger but that season we sold him to Millwall because their manager and my old friend Jimmy Nicholl offered us a really good deal that we just couldn't afford to turn down.

I was eventually appointed manager in September 1996. As soon as Iain announced he was leaving the chairman, David Campbell, offered me the job. It was a really tight ship we had at Hamilton; we had the chairman, Alastair Duguid, Scott Struthers the secretary and Margaret Montgomery and that was basically the infrastructure of the club away from the playing staff. Margaret, or 'Big Mags' as we called her, was absolutely brilliant. We used to train in the morning and then we would go to the Hamilton Accies Social Club for our lunch. 'Big Mags' always did the catering for all the boys. She produced large-scale lunches with the minimum of stuff. She was first class, it was just as well because everything at the club was done on a shoestring. The crowds were minimal and we had next to no money because we didn't have our own ground. Everybody at the club mucked in and did what we could and that brought a real togetherness.

I also turned forty when I was at Accies. I was never really a big one for birthday parties, I had never had one in my life before but the boys arranged a special surprise for me in the social club. Some of the bar staff used to complain about the players and the mess they left after their lunches. It had started to get to me. I was sitting in the office, on my birthday, when Scott Struthers came into the office and said, 'The boys are getting a hard time again. The boys are cracking up. You better come down and sort it.' I was absolutely raging and I raced downstairs to give the staff what for but when I walked into the room I realised I had been set up. The players had got me a stripper for my birthday, they had done me like a kipper. The stripper was dressed up in a police uniform and I have to admit I have never been so embarrassed in all my life. Margaret and all the boys had all been in on the act. I will never forget it and they all better remember I still owe them.

The Saturday after that we played away against Berwick Rangers. We won the match 2–0 but there were a number of things I wasn't happy with. I ripped into the boys after the game, I felt they had been too sloppy and there could have been far more goals in the game. You can imagine that the bus journey back up from Berwick was hardly the best, despite the result. The bus ended up dropping me off at Bathgate on the way back to Hamilton. After a game, when I got back, I used to go for a pint in my local, the Kaim Park in Bathgate, with Gary Brown, who used to be at Hearts, and Archie Meikle. I normally just waited there until my wife, Liz, came and picked me up. I was waiting and waiting and ended up having a few but I didn't really want to drink because I was still annoyed with the way the team had played. Archie, who was married at the time, then came up to me and said, 'Can you help me? I've got a problem. I've been having an affair with this girl who just walked into the bar and she is looking for me.' I couldn't believe what he had just told me, Archie isn't the sort of person who would have an affair. I completely panicked and grabbed Archie and dragged him out the bar and into the big hallway, I had never sobered up so quickly in all my life. I then looked up the corridor and saw all my family, all our friends and the entire Hamilton team waiting to give me a surprise fortieth birthday party. The team bus had gone back to Hamilton to pick up the wives and girlfriends and had then doubled back to drop them all off again. I felt absolutely awful, as I had spent most of the afternoon absolutely slaughtering them. It ended up a good night and I had to say sorry a few times before the end of it. The event was organised and arranged by 'Big Mags' and aided and abetted by Liz. Also Archie's performance that night in stitching me up was worthy of an Oscar.

Berwick's Shielfield Park turned out to be a lucky stomping ground for Hamilton that season. We won 5–0 there to clinch promotion, in a game where Paul Ritchie grabbed a hat-trick. The *Daily Record* ran a competition that season. It was a race to see what player could get to thirty goals first – with the winner getting a big bottle of whisky. Paul got to thirty-first, in a game away to Dumbarton, but the paper didn't want to give him the prize so I had to intervene on his behalf. I ended up cracking up with them but they were trying to hold off and give it to a more high-profile SPL star, like Jorge Cadete, Brian Laudrup or Ally McCoist. After some gentle persuasion the *Daily Record* eventually relented and Paul got his prize. Paul lacked confidence when he first came but he turned into a really big player for us, and his goals were certainly vital for us that season as we won promotion.

Ayr United ended up winning the league. Gordon Dalziel was their manager, he had spent an absolute fortune that season and really should have won the league at a canter. In the end, they did finish top and ended up as worthy champions. We pushed them bravely all the way and finished only three points behind. What ended up costing us was our head-to-head record, we just couldn't beat Ayr that season and that proved to be the difference.

It was still a decent feat to win promotion. That Hamilton team were a good and honest bunch and we had some real char-acters in that squad, including three part-timers in Paul 'Wolfie' McKenzie, Steve 'Steish' Thomson and Crawford Baptie. I would train the full-time players during the day and the part-time boys at night. I was still reasonably fit at the time and we would head off running in the dark at Strathclyde or Chatelherault Park most nights.

Gary Clark was another experienced player. He was a great lad and I was really shocked when he was linked with the Tommy Sheridan scandal. Gary is one of the nicest guys I have come across in the game. I really felt for him when he hit the head-lines. I still bump into him at social events and we always have a good chat about the good times we had at Accies. He is a top bloke.

Scott 'Bob' McCulloch was a defender we signed from Rangers. He did really well and we ended up selling him to Dunfermline. Scott came to us a bit overweight and had fallen out of love with the game, but with a bit of gentle persuasion and some hard work we got Scott and his career back on track. He moved back up to the top level again. Success stories like Scott make it all worthwhile.

Jose Quitongo was another character. He had been on trial down south and through one of Iain Munro's contacts he managed to get Jose up to Hamilton, right away we could see he had something – but he also was sadly lacking in other areas. He was quick and could do some amazing things but other times he looked like he had never seen a football. Early on he struggled to even kick the ball any distance. When it came to long shots or crossing the ball he was just a complete waste of space. I took him for a session and we were playing balls for him to run on to and cross. A simple exercise, could he do it? No. I don't think he managed to do it once. The ball would trundle into the box, out of the park or he would end up falling on his backside. We just kept working at Jose until he eventually got there. The great thing about Jose is he is such an infectious character. There were times when his antics would leave us both in hysterics. He always has a smile on his face. He played for Hearts before he returned for another couple of spells with Accies and certainly did well for himself. It is something I might have questioned having seen him when he first arrived in Scottish football.

The club really started to struggle. If it hadn't been for David Campbell continually putting money into the club then I hate to think where Accies would have ended up. It was good to give him some return for his money and something to celebrate with our promotion back to the First Division.

The ownership of the club was very complex. The director Robert Gibb passed away and his shares were automatically transferred. It saw David Campbell ousted as chairman when we were back in the First Division, David Gebbie came in as the new chairman and Bill Sherry took over as chief executive. I was sad to see Alastair Duguid and David Campbell go because I really enjoyed working for them. The last thing I needed was another boardroom change after everything that had gone on at Hearts. I was determined I wasn't going to be messed about again. I had learned some valuable lessons and basically laid things on the line. I said, 'If you want the club to be successful then this is how I want things to be done.' I was fortunate because I was in a position of strength after we had won promotion. I have to say that neither David nor Bill ever questioned anything. They were unbelievably supportive, they couldn't do enough to help and they also gave me a new contract on improved terms. If I am being honest, the contract was probably too rich for the First Division. They showed a lot of faith in me and even wanted me to become a director and go on to the board, but I declined. I didn't feel it was the right thing to do because I wanted to focus solely on the management side.

I managed to keep Accies in the First Division. It was a struggle but we managed to finish just above the relegation positions with Partick Thistle and Stirling Albion going down. The job I was doing at Hamilton didn't go unnoticed. I remember the day St Johnstone made their approach. Paul Sturrock left to join Dundee United but I had absolutely no idea I was on their radar to replace him. It was a Friday morning, I had just come back from training and Bill Sherry chapped on the door and asked me to come into his office. I walked into his office and Scott Struthers and he were standing there ashen faced. I looked at them and said, 'Going by my past experiences of this type of situation it looks like I am going to be sacked.' Then Bill said, 'Geoff Brown [the St Johnstone chairman] has been on the phone. He wants to speak to you about going to St Johnstone. It is entirely up to you if you want to speak to them but we don't want you to go.' I had never stood in the way of any of my Hamilton players when they had been given the chance to better themselves and I knew this was a good opportunity that I would have to seriously consider. It was back in the Premier Division and St Johnstone were also a good, well-run club.

The St Johnstone chief executive Stewart Duff phoned me and told me the clubs had agreed compensation and would I meet the chairman and him in Glasgow? We had a game against Ayr United that day and the story had come out in the press. The players were all asking what was happening. I told them that I hadn't made up my mind but I was going to be meeting with St Johnstone later that night. I met Geoff and Stewart. Geoff told me he simply wanted St Johnstone to be the best they could be. He never set any wild goals or told me that he wanted this trophy or that trophy. I got a good feeling from the meeting, talks went well and I had virtually all but agreed to take the job.

I went home that night and spoke to Liz and the kids. The

one thing that was unsettling me was that I was really happy at Hamilton. If I walked away from Accies would I get the same pleasure at St Johnstone? I had a good squad of players, a board who backed me and together the club was one tight unit. I had a meal and a few glasses of wine and later on that Saturday night I remember I said to Liz, 'That is it. I'm not going. I enjoy it too much at Hamilton.' Thankfully I never said it publicly to anybody. It was a combination of the alcohol kicking in, my emotions and the strong feelings and emotions I had towards Hamilton. But once my head had cleared in the morning there was only one decision I could make and that was to go to Perth.

Hamilton were suddenly looking for my replacement and I recommended my former Hearts teammate and captain Craig Levein for the job. He had retired early because of injury and had already taken his first step on to the management ladder with Cowdenbeath. The Accies board interviewed Craig but, unbelievably, never gave him the job. Instead they elected to give it to the former Hamilton player and Canadian international Colin Miller. I think he still remains their most capped player and it was maybe an easy appointment because he had a connection to the club and was a fans' favourite but I still don't know how Craig never got the job. The Hamilton board of that time must look back on that decision with absolute disbelief. Craig went on to manage Hearts, in England and the Scottish national team. Craig has shown he has what it takes while the Accies board went for Miller and his time at the club ended up being a total disaster. If the Hamilton directors knew then what they do today then I am sure they would have made a very different decision.

23

WHEN THE SAINTS GO MARCHING IN

MY FIRST game in charge of St Johnstone was a League Cup quarter-final clash against Hibs on 8 September 1998. It couldn't have gone any better as my new team thrashed Hibs 4–0. A Nathan Lowndes double and goals from Gerry McMahon and John O'Neil did the damage and booked our place in the semi-finals. It wasn't a bad way to start my McDiarmid Park career, although the St Johnstone players have to take all the credit for the way they played, they simply blew Hibs away. I was delighted with the result although I have to admit that I did feel more than a slight sense of guilt because the manager of Hibs that night was Alex McLeish, the same man who had helped me get back into the game at Motherwell, after I had been sacked by Hearts. That League Cup game took care of itself and it set up a clash with Hearts in the semi-final. There was a lot to look forward to, but before that there were some important league games.

I still had to get to know my players and to get a handle on them. I spoke to Paul Sturrock before I took the job and he was great. He gave me his opinions on the squad and what their strengths and weaknesses were. I certainly didn't have many complaints about the squad I inherited and I went into the job confident I could do well. I had done a decent job at Hamilton and at Hearts and I was desperate to make my mark on my long-awaited return to the Scottish Premier Division with St

Johnstone. That cup win over Hibs was the start of a really good spell for the club.

I know a lot of people will say that it was Paul Sturrock's team. In a sense it was because he had signed most of the players, but in that sort of situation it can be a lot harder for a new manager because you have to win over the trust of your squad and try to convince them to buy into your plans and philosophies. It is not always that easy, as I had found out at Partick Thistle. The good thing about that St Johnstone squad was that they were a decent team and also had a lot of good professionals into the bargain. We seemed to bond quite well from the off and it helped that we had started promisingly, with a draw against Dunfermline and a win against Aberdeen.

It also took me a couple of weeks to get my own assistant manager in place. This time I finally managed to get Billy Kirkwood, at the second time of asking, after he had knocked me back at Hearts. Billy had been down at Hull City, assisting Mark Hateley, but the good thing for me was that the Kirkwood family was still based in Perth. Billy proved to be a really good appointment for me and together with the team we went from strength to strength.

The early highlight was our 1–0 win at Celtic Park, thanks to Nick Dasovic's goal. The club had a dreadful record at Parkhead but we went to Glasgow and put in a very disciplined team performance and ran out worthy winners. That result, not surprisingly, boosted the confidence and belief that we could achieve something special. Bizarrely, we then suffered our first defeat to Paul Sturrock's Dundee United, although we managed to grab a 1–1 draw against Hearts at Tynecastle. My return to Gorgie was one I was really looking forward to. I always get a good reception from the Hearts fans, who remember my time there, as a player, coach and manager.

We kept the momentum going by thrashing Motherwell 5–0, in what was the first game of my former Rangers teammate, Billy Davies, in charge of the Fir Park outfit. It proved the perfect preparation for our semi-final with Hearts. It was a night that I will never forget, I went into that game full of confidence because I believed in the players. My trust wasn't to be misplaced because the team was absolutely brilliant on the night. We won the match 3–0, thanks to some spectacular finishing from Allan Preston, Nick Dasovic and George O'Boyle. We were 2–0 up at half-time and I knew then we were never going to lose. The final whistle left me with a real feeling of satisfaction, not because we had beaten Hearts but more the fact St Johnstone had made it to a major cup final. The fact I had got one over my former Hearts chairman Chris Robinson was secondary.

We were on a good run and that pretty much continued throughout that campaign. I felt confident going into every match that we were good enough to win. We never really changed the formation or the system too much. It was a straight 4–4–2 but I had so many guys who could fill a number of positions and offer us some versatility. John O'Neil could play as a striker, central midfielder or as a winger. Nathan Lowndes could step in wide or as a centre forward and Nick Dasovic and Paul Kane both got forward from the midfield. We also had the Portuguese striker Miguel Simao, who Paul Sturrock had signed from Aves, and my initial thoughts of him were far from favourable. He was quick and skilful but I thought he was too soft and not determined enough for the Scottish game. Even Miguel would admit he found our football something of a culture shock, but as soon as he adapted he showed he was a player of extreme talent. I spent a lot of time with him on the training park and, to be fair to him, he worked hard on his game. He became an outstanding player at St Johnstone and a hero to the fans. Gerry

McMahon was another quick winger and so we had a lot of options going forward, including George O'Boyle, Philip Scott and Allan Preston. Roddy Grant was also a fans' favourite. He couldn't run but had incredible ability and scored a lot of important goals for us.

We also had a good solid base from which to push on from, Alan Main was a magnificent goalkeeper and he had a settled back four in front of him. The former Republic of Ireland star Alan Kernaghan and Darren Dods were the centre halves. I hope that Darren now appreciates how good Alan was. Alan was a top-level defender. He was also a good guy in the dressing room and all the boys used to rib big Darren because Alan would always be telling him what to do on the pitch. He would shout run, jump, head and Darren would just go and do it. Alan was right so often. Darren Dods has also had a half-decent career and I am sure looking back even he will agree that he learned so much from playing alongside Alan. We also had the young Northern Irish international Danny Griffin as cover along with John McQuillan and Gary Bollan in the full back positions. We had a good mixture of youth and experience, mixed with organisation and flair.

We were more than a match for anybody in the Scottish Premier League. The only team we really found it hard against was Rangers. My former club had spent big money in backing their new manager, Dick Advocaat, as he looked to build on Walter Smith's Ibrox dynasty. It was that open cheque-book approach that was later to come back and haunt Rangers, when they were forced to go into administration at the start of 2012. They had substantial debts and the club also had a massive tax bill hanging over them, as a result of a controversial loophole that had seen them pay some of their player wages into overseas accounts. It was a move that would see both the players and the club pay less tax and made Rangers a far more attractive proposition to Europe's top stars, but in the end Her Majesty's Revenue and Customs came calling.

Rangers went out and bought genuine quality like Giovanni van Bronckhorst, Arthur Numan, Andrei Kanchelskis and Gabriel Amato. They were a class above every other team in the league and that was shown the day they thrashed us 7–0 at McDiarmid Park. Paul Kane got sent off early and Rangers brutally put us to the sword. It was made even worse as our humiliation was beamed live to the nation via Sky Television. I remember standing on the touchline, suffering like every other St Johnstone supporter, thinking, 'I know we are getting hammered, but I don't think we have played that badly.' If I had said that publicly then I know I would have been carted away by the men in white coats. I went home and watched the match again and the re-run backed me up, we hadn't been as bad as the scoreline had suggested. We had created a right few chances and Kane had been unlucky to be red-carded. Rangers had been absolutely devastating with the goals they had scored but we had also played well in spells. My only concern was that the defeat didn't dent confidence. It didn't help that in our next game we were playing the other half of the Old Firm. Celtic had a good team although they weren't in Rangers' class and we had already beaten them on their own patch. We sat down as a team, watched the video and I went to great lengths to stress to the players all the positives and things they had done well against Rangers. It seemed to work as they were bright and bubbly in training all that week and there was a real buzz around the squad. The chief executive Stewart Duff also joked that week saying, 'We'll find out this week whether or not you are a good manager.' He was half-serious and half-joking. He wasn't being nasty, he was just making a point. Thankfully, my confidence wasn't misplaced because we went out and beat Celtic 2–1, with John O'Neil and Kieran McAnespie getting our goals. It left me with a very comforting feeling because I believed, and so did the players, that the 7–0 was a real one-off. They went out and showed that was the case.

We continued our good form with a win at Aberdeen and then turned our attentions to the League Cup final. I looked at the Rangers squad and then ourselves. I just thought to myself we should have absolutely no chance. It might have sounded a bit pessimistic but after the 7–0 defeat we knew how devastating Rangers could be. I had to make the players believe they could do it because there is no point in going into a game unless you believe you can do something. We knew it was going to be hard and we would need to play to our maximum and hope Rangers had an off day. The boys were also really fired up because of what had happened in the 7–0 game and because they were also potentially ninety minutes away from lifting a major cup.

We acquitted ourselves well and gave as good as we got although Rangers went ahead through a Stephane Guivarc'h goal, but we refused to let the heads go down and got a well-deserved equaliser through Nick Dasovic. We hung in there but eventually lost out to a late Jorg Albertz goal. We tried to get back into the game but couldn't dig out a second equaliser.

In hindsight, I maybe should have picked a different team for the final. George O'Boyle and Allan Preston had been in and out of the team with injuries but they had both played their part in the cup run and had also scored goals in the semi-final win over Hearts. I wasn't sure whether or not to play them so I put Allan on the bench and started with George, but I probably should have named George amongst the substitutes as well because he wasn't as fit as he should have been. I knew what a quality player he was, but I probably should have gone for Nathan Lowndes because of his pace and energy. He would have got more change out of the Rangers defence. That might have been a mistake I had made in picking my starting XI. The team certainly didn't let the club or Perth down but it was still a hard one to stomach. I remember standing on the Celtic Park pitch watching the Rangers players celebrating with their fans and for me and all the St Johnstone players it was a really lonely feeling. I was really disappointed and I thought to myself, 'I hope I never have to stomach another cup final defeat again in my life.' Losing a cup final was far worse as a manager than it was as a player. Playing you are out on the park and you have an influence on things but as a manager you are in the hands of your team. I don't think the boys could have given me much more but I was left with a real empty feeling after that cup final.

We bounced back to hold our own in the league and we kept ourselves very much in the hunt for European football. We had three away games in a row, around the March, when we played Dundee, Motherwell and Hearts in the Scottish Cup. We managed to win all three games and our next match was at home against Kilmarnock. We were really looking for a big crowd because we knew if we won we would go third in the league, but only 5,461 fans turned out and that really sickened the chairman, Geoff Brown, big time and you can understand why. I think he realised then that St Johnstone weren't going to get too much more of a support. It was a bit of a let-down because nobody at the club could have done any more. We were having success on the field, but the majority of the Perth public didn't get behind us. I am not knocking the St Johnstone fans because they still have a real core of fans who travel the length and breadth of the country cheering their team on through thick and thin. They are a loyal bunch but the club deserves a bigger support.

That season they had plenty to cheer about. We also managed to put our Rangers hoodoo to bed as we beat them 3–1 at

McDiarmid Park with Kieran McAnespie, Miguel Simao and Jim Weir all on target. I managed to strike up a good friendship with the Rangers manager Dick Advocaat. He was very complimentary of the St Johnstone team and also thanked me at the end of the season for beating Celtic and making his job a little easier. The ironic thing over the course of that season was we beat Celtic three times, but we still had unfinished business of our own.

The race for third place went down to a straight fight between Kilmarnock and ourselves. We had to go down to Rugby Park on the second last game of the season and more than 15,000 fans turned out at Rugby Park because it was a massive game for both teams. We went into the game knowing that if we lost Kilmarnock would seal third place. The good thing for us was that we knew if we avoided defeat then things could be back in our hands on the final day because we had Dundee, albeit it was a local derby, while Kilmarnock had to go to Ibrox to take on Rangers. It was Kilmarnock who scored first through Mark Roberts and went in 1–0 up at the break. I had a choice: Do I go into the dressing room and not say much and hope the players pick themselves up or do I go in and have a right go at them? I decided to go for the latter and read them the riot act. The game was far too important for us just to throw in the towel, we had done all the hard work and I didn't want it to simply peter out. I let rip and gave a few of them a hard time. I said stuff like 'Are you going to bottle it now?' and 'You need to give it everything you have got because if you don't take anything today then you can forget about third spot.' The players got it in the neck individually and collectively and it had the desired effect because Gary Bollan got an equaliser and we ended up drawing 1–1.

It meant that if we beat Dundee and Rangers took care of Kilmarnock then we would finish in third place. It was an amazing day. McDiarmid Park was sold out and it was some game. It was a tense and nervous affair and we eventually came out on top thanks to a Paul Kane header in the second half, while Rangers played their part by holding Kilmarnock to a draw at Ibrox. It was a tremendous feat for St Johnstone to clinch third spot because we had punched above our weight and finished above teams who had spent a lot more than we had.

I was also delighted Paul got the goal. He was a good player to have around and with Paul being a Hibee and me being a Hearts man it added a bit of spice to our relationship. After the game the celebrations kicked in and Paul turned and started having a go at me. He said, 'What about you last week, at half-time in the Kilmarnock game? I was ready to swing for you, you really, really annoyed me.' I said to him something along the lines of, 'Well, how did you play in the second half and did it work?' He eventually agreed that it had and we ended up having a laugh and joke about things and got back to celebrating the fact that St Johnstone had finished third in the league.

Football has certainly changed a lot since my playing days, now you have to treat players with kid gloves. I was brought up with rough and ready people, who called a spade a spade and I don't think it did me any harm. There are times when you have to lay down the law to get the best out of your players – but now there has to be more of a balance.

Still on the subject of Mr Kane, I actually tried to sign Paul when I was Hearts manager. He was at Aberdeen at the time, but he refused point-blank to even consider going to Tynecastle, he was just too much of a Hibee.

Every St Johnstone fan will remember Paul's goal from that Dundee game, but our goalkeeper, Alan Main, also had a big part in that win. Alan had a save from James Grady at 0–0 that was out of this world. I still remember his stop. Grady fired a volley right into the top corner and Alan had no right to save it but somehow managed to get a hand to it. It is quality like that which so often can be the difference between success and failure. That season certainly turned out to be a big one for St Johnstone.

Looking back we got to the cup final, the semi-final of the Scottish Cup and finished third in the league, which brought a European return. For me, it would stand up as one of the best seasons in St Johnstone's history. It was my first season and one I look back on with a great sense of achievement. I am still really proud of what we did that season but I have to say that I don't feel that team gets the recognition it deserves. That season is never really mentioned or brought up as often as I think it should be.

24

HIGH-ROLLING IN MONACO AND GAMBLING ON CHANGE

THE 1999–2000 season was always going to be a big one for St Johnstone. Our prize for finishing third was a place in the UEFA Cup and that brought a real buzz of excitement. Saints had only played in Europe once before and twenty-eight years later we made our triumphant return to the UEFA Cup. We were drawn against the Finnish team VPS Vaasa. I went out to see them play and was confident we could get past them. We went over to Finland for the first game and they proved a tough nut to crack. You look at games in Europe and go and watch teams and think your team can beat them, but until they are up against your own players then that is the only time you can get an exact gauge of European opposition. Vaasa were competent but they were no world beaters, and we drew 1–1 over there. They went ahead although we missed umpteen chances and Vaasa defended for their lives before we finally got our equaliser when Nathan Lowndes came off the bench to save us. We could have won the game at the death but they managed to scramble an effort from Roddy Grant off the line, but it had been a hard, hard night. The good thing was that we hadn't lost and had managed to get an invaluable away goal.

I was confident we could still progress but I knew it would still be difficult, especially if we lost a goal. The McDiarmid Park return was a tense affair and we had to show patience again. I gave Lowndes a start after his heroics in the away leg but it didn't happen for him, or the team, so I took him off with ten minutes to go and sent on Miguel Simao. The substitution worked as Miguel scored two late goals to put us through.

That put us into the next round and that was where the real glamour came. We were drawn with the French millionaires from Monaco. They had some team and boasted footballing super-stars like David Trezeguet, Fabien Barthez, John-Arne Riise and Marco Simeone. Their squad was like a 'Who's Who?' of European football. It was bad enough facing up to Rangers or Celtic but on paper Monaco were even more formidable. Their undoubted ability was shown by the fact they had reached the semi-final of the Champions League two seasons earlier, so this was a team that was still very much at its peak. Even away from their head-line acts they were able to call on players with the class of Willy Sagnol, Ludovic Guily, Rafa Marquez, Sylvain Legwinski, Phillipe Christanval and Dado Prso, who later went on to star for Rangers. The Monaco coach Claude Puel's biggest headache would have been keeping all his squad happy because he certainly couldn't have got them all in his starting XI.

I went to see Monaco play in Rennes while our scout, Athole Henderson, watched them again before our own trip to the Stade Louis II. We did our homework on them although their quality was there for all to see; they were a top team. These are the sort of games where you know nine times out of ten you are going to have no chance but we had to cling on to the belief that it could happen.

I had to make our players believe that on a one-off occasion they could match Monaco, despite their multi-million pound transfer fees and bulging wage packets. They might have had some of Europe's elite, but these guys weren't miles better than your average footballer. There wasn't that big a gap. There might have been in terms of consistency but not always in skill levels. Neil Berry, who I played with at Hearts, was the perfect example. He would play to his strengths game after game but with your so-called flair players you might only get one performance in every four or five games. I had a nucleus of a team where I knew seven or eight of my players would give me everything they had, regardless of how they were playing. If you do that then you are never going to be too far away. That was the way it was at St Johnstone. The back four and goalkeeper never gave much away, we had experience in the middle of the park with Paul Kane and Nick Dasovic and that gave us a good, solid spine. All I was doing was tinkering with the front positions and continually working on the mental side of things, making the players believe they could compete and beat the best. Such psychology can also work the other way, I have seen it happen, when players are constantly hammered and told they will never make it. Some people start to believe that as well so you have to strike a balance. You have to give your teams belief and hope it rubs off out on the pitch.

Going into that game in Monaco we found ourselves under siege and our goalkeeper Alan Main played like a man possessed. We went in 0–0 at half-time and then had a great chance when Miguel Simao went one-on-one with the goalkeeper, Fabien Barthez, but he missed. I have to say that if I wanted any of my players to have been in that position then it would have been Miguel, but it wasn't to be that night. In the end, a double from Italian international Marco Simone and another from the French superstar David Trezeguet killed us off.

We knew then the tie was all but over but we still had to try and salvage some pride from the McDiarmid Park return. The match was brought forward to 5pm to accommodate French television. We got off to the perfect start when we went ahead early through an own goal from Philippe Leonard, but then Dado Prso and John-Arne Riise scored to kill our dream stone dead. Canadian star Nick Dasovic pulled us level and then we should have had been given a penalty for a Fabien Barthez challenge on Miguel Simao but our cast-iron claims were ignored. Insult was then added to injury when Sylvain Legwinski scored for the French visitors before John O'Neil equalised to help us save some face. It also meant I had managed to maintain St Johnstone's unbeaten home run in Europe. The club and players were happy because they showed over the course of ninety minutes that they could compete with the best. The club had also made quite a bit of money from the two Monaco games as the French television channel Canal+ had shown both games and so, all in all, it had been a worthwhile adventure for St Johnstone.

The club were in a decent financial position and to be fair to chairman Geoff Brown he made funds available to me. Geoff never once stopped me from signing anyone. We tried to sign Jim Hamilton from Hearts not long after I had arrived in Perth. We agreed a substantial fee but Jim knocked us back and decided he wanted to stay at Tynecastle.

We had lost Philip Scott to Sheffield Wednesday at the end of my first season. I had earmarked the young Celtic playmaker John-Paul McBride as his replacement. John-Paul is one signing I take a lot criticism for. I paid a lot of money for him and Geoff backed me all the way in that deal. I think Geoff also spoke to a Celtic director who gave John-Paul a good reference, telling him he was getting a good player for the money he was paying. I looked at John-Paul football-wise and saw he was a young talent coming through. He was a young player with incredible ability, but he just had too many hang-ups and not enough desire to make it at the top level. His family background didn't help and he had other issues, which I felt held him back. He came in to training one day after Celtic had beaten Rangers and he had this massive Celtic tattoo that covered his entire back. That is fine; support your team by all means, but when you are playing for another team then I don't think getting a massive tattoo of a rival team is the most sensible thing to do. Don't get me wrong, he was still a smashing, young lad but he didn't have that mental toughness and focus to fulfil the unquestionable talent he had.

I also tried to strengthen our striking options when I brought Graeme Jones in from Wigan Athletic. Graeme has fond memories of his time at St Johnstone although I know he is disappointed he never scored more goals. Graeme is so tight that he still has his first pound in his pocket, but he was a good professional and player. He is now a well-respected coach and assistant manager to Roberto Martinez back at Wigan Athletic. Sticking up for Graeme also saw me come near to blows with the Motherwell manager and my ex-teammate Billy Davies. It came in a game we lost 1–0 at Fir Park, after Graeme had been sent off. Graeme should have known better but he was getting constantly baited by the Motherwell players, who were being wound up by Billy Davies. I knew Billy well, but our friend-ship went out the window that afternoon. I told him in no uncertain terms what I thought of his antics. After the game I was still furious and went looking for him but he sprinted up the tunnel, he didn't even shake my hand and I didn't see him again after the game – maybe it was just as well he stayed out of the way. Everything is fine now and it was just one of those things that happen in football. He thought he was in the right and I didn't and things got heated, which is all part of the passion of the game.

Craig Russell was another striker we paid a bit of money for to buy from Manchester City, after a successful loan spell at

McDiarmid Park. I thought he would be a good addition to our squad but he struggled. I also signed Kevin Thomas for £100,000 from Morton. I knew him well and felt he would be a good signing, having worked with him at Hearts. Young Keigan Parker came through the ranks too, and I gave him his debut at sixteen. He was a youngster who developed into a top-class player.

We also signed Martin Lauchlan for £50,000 from Partick Thistle. The chairman came and asked me about him. The club had an excess and I was told they had to spend it otherwise they would have to pay most of it out in tax, so the chairman asked me if I fancied Martin. He was a young winger who I had seen a couple of times and wasn't too bad but he wouldn't have been one of the first names on my list. He said, 'I can get him,' and I said, 'Well, do it because he could do us a turn and maybe strengthen the squad.' Unfortunately, it didn't work out as he didn't quite have what it took to make a name for himself in the top league.

I made quite a few changes and signings although we also helped to balance the books by selling Danny Griffin who we sold for £650,000 to Dundee United. He was unfortunate that he wasn't playing in the team every week and it was only because my back four, of John McQuillan, Alan Kernaghan, Darren Dods and Gary Bollan, were so solid and settled. Danny would come in when any of them were missing and fill any position across the back line or even as a holding midfielder. He was a good player and a Northern Irish cap. I also have to give Geoff Brown a lot of credit because he did the negotiations for that transfer with United and got a very good deal for St Johnstone. Geoff had a really close relationship with Paul Sturrock and they managed to strike that deal between them. I felt we were losing a good player but we were getting good money for Danny, especially as Geoff had managed to push the transfer fee up a fair bit.

It ended up being a season of change but we managed to finish fifth in the Scottish Premier League. We had slipped a couple of places but it should still have been seen as a season of success for St Johnstone. I still think when you are as high as that, with the budget we had, then we really were punching above our weight. Motherwell and Hearts had both jumped above us but had both splashed out lavishly to strengthen their respective squads. They got their just rewards as a result.

25

HARTLEY AND SYLLA DESTINED
FOR BROWN'S BIN

WE HAD maintained exceptionally high standards in my first two campaigns at St Johnstone, but with every passing season it became more and more of a challenge to hit those dizzy heights. The biggest bugbear for me was the introduction of the Bosman Ruling. It allowed players over the age of twenty-three to move on freedom of contract to other countries and you could join another team in your country if you were over twenty-four. It was great for the players and the big clubs but I would have to question how much it actually helped teams, like ourselves, who were operating at the opposite end of the spectrum. I would say it hit us harder than most, especially at the start of the 2000–01 season.

We lost two of our top players, John O'Neil and John McQuillan, under the Bosman Ruling. O'Neil went to Hibs and McQuillan teamed up with Paul Sturrock again at Dundee United. They had been two of our top performers over the previous couple of seasons and suddenly we had lost them for nothing. That is the price of success. The team had done well and being a major part of that brought both Johns to the attentions of others. We fought hard to keep them but we were always fighting a losing battle. We made them decent offers, by St Johnstone standards, but we couldn't get anywhere near what was being offered from some of our Premier League rivals. I could have talked to them until I was blue in the face, telling them they would have been better staying at St Johnstone, but who could blame the boys for taking the best offers they could get. It is a short career and playing at most clubs, outside of the Old Firm, means you are unlikely to be made beyond your playing days, so these boys went with my best wishes. They all had families to support and mortgages to pay and I could understand their reasons for going but I was still sad and disappointed to see them leave. It made my job even harder, having to replace quality like that for nothing. Keith O'Halloran was another we tried to keep but he also left that same summer, joining Swindon Town on freedom of contract, while I also let Gerry McMahon return to Northern Ireland.

I needed to strengthen again and I signed Paul Hartley from Hibs. I had known Paul since he was a sixteen-year-old at Hamilton. He was a really good player, although by his own admission he didn't play the best football of his career at St Johnstone. He got sent off in a game against St Mirren and in other early games he was up and down. It takes time for players to bed in and Paul had come through some difficult times at Millwall and Raith Rovers and things hadn't worked out for him at Hibs either and Paul was trying to find his feet again. It was around Christmas and my wife, Liz, was sitting in the stand and Geoff came up to her and said, 'I am going to buy Sandy a bin for his Christmas and make sure Hartley goes in it. He is rubbish!' Geoff, to be fair, also said something similar to me about Paul. I was disappointed and anybody who knows me will be aware that my loyalty was always to my players. When you have seen the way Paul's career has gone since he left McDiarmid Park, going to Hearts, playing in the Champions League for Celtic and also starring for Scotland, it shows just what a special talent he was. I always knew he could be a top player and was in no

Me as a happy Hammer.

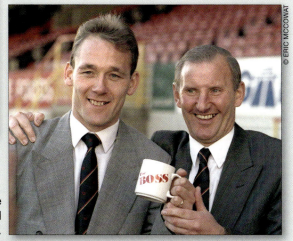

Appointed Partick Thistle manager alongside my old Airdrie boss Bobby Watson.

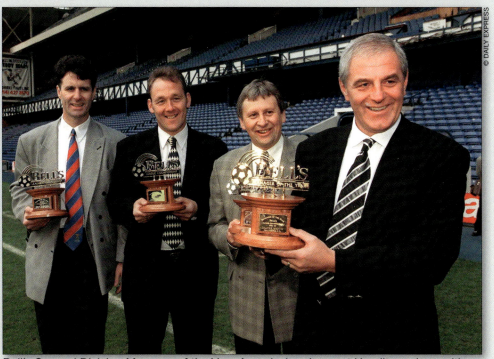

Bell's Second Division Manager of the Year Award when I was at Hamilton, along with fellow divisional winners, Rangers boss Walter Smith, Inverness's Steve Paterson and St Johnstone's Paul Sturrock.

Welcoming the great Pelé to Tynecastle.

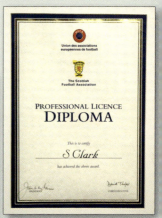

My UEFA pro-licence – Europe's top coaching award.

My young Hearts team that won the BP Youth Cup. (Back row: Paul Ritchie, Allan McManus, Gordon Connolly, Mark Bradley, Myles Hogarth, Kevin Thomas, Grant Duncan. Front row: Colin Walker, Grant Murray, Gary Locke, Paul Weatherston, Stuart Callaghan, David Murie.)

A derby from the dugout.

Wayne Foster nets his famous winner for me against Hibs

The legendary Fozzie goal celebration.

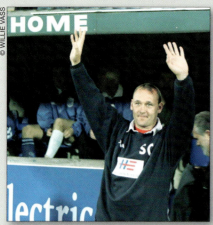

My McDiarmid Park bow.

Celebrating making the League Cup final with our semi-final win over Hearts.

Paul Kane nets the final day winner against Dundee that seals third spot for St Johnstone.

Unwanted headlines – as George O'Boyle and Kevin Thomas make the papers for all the wrong reasons.

Leading the celebrations at the final whistle as Saints get ready to return to Europe.

Nathan Lowndes celebrates his goal against Vaasa.

Nathan Lowndes challenges for the ball with Monaco's Bruno Irles, with the legendary Rafa Marquez's watching on.

Miguel Simao scores the goal that puts out Vaasa.

My Saints backroom team - Athole Henderson, Nick Summersgill, Jocky Peebles, Billy Kirkwood and myself in Monaco.

Joining Jimmy Calderwood at Dunfermline.

Aberdeen's Sone Aluko takes on Bayern Munich star Christian Lell.

Hampden disappointment as Aberdeen lose Scottish Cup semi-final to Queen of the South.

The Kilmarnock dugout celebrate our final day survival win over Falkirk.

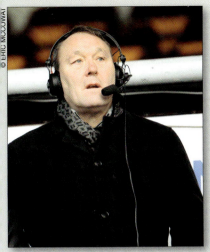

On air with the BBC.

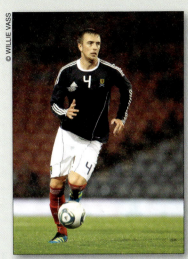

Danny Wilson
starring for Scotland.

Spot the stars? - That all conquering Murieston Boys Club team. (Back row: Devon Jacobs, Sam Strathie, Danny Wilson, Darren Jamieson, Gavin Davis, Darren Cole, Sheldon Jacobs, Front row: Rhys McCabe, Kevin Mochan, Stephen Fleming, Kyle Jacobs, Mark Sharpe, Nicky Clark, Paul O'Day.)

The Cumbernauld College team – Jamie Dempsey, Ally Britton, Sean Tough, Davie Mitchell and Todd Lumsden, with Davie Hay and myself in the front row.

Liz and I on our wedding day.

Nicky at Queen of the South.

Suzi on the day of her graduation.

Gary during his passing out parade.

Nicky, Liz, Suzi and I flank Gary on the day of his passing out parade.

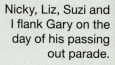

doubt Paul had the quality to play at the top level but I just wonder if Geoff Brown would now be man enough to hold up his hands and say he was wrong about him.

Momo Sylla came into the equation as we searched for a right back to replace John McQuillan. Agents throw a million names at you and you need to try and filter them down. We were also trying to get players in for next to nothing. Momo came in on trial in the summer of 2000, after he had left Le Mans. He was from Guinea and hardly spoke a word of English. There was a bit of a language barrier with his lack of English and my French being even worse, but I still got a good feeling about Momo. He showed up well in training and then played a couple of trial games. Right away I thought this guy is a player. He was big, strong and quick and he could do some amazing things with the ball. I was initially looking for a right-back but Momo could play there, midfield or as a striker. Normally over the course of a game he would end up playing in all these positions – usually of his own accord, I have to add.

I signed Momo but I quickly found out he was a bit of a free spirit. He loved to disappear back to Paris whenever he could. He was undisciplined at times on and off the pitch, he would do some brilliant things and in the next moment you would see him standing at the halfway line with his hands on his hips, having not even bothered to have chased his man back. That was just Momo, but for all the mayhem you always knew there could be some magic. There was a game in October 2000 when we beat Rangers 2–1. It was the match where Dick Advocaat came out and slaughtered his team, calling them big heads. He was right, Rangers hadn't been at their best, but a lot of that was down to how well my St Johnstone boys had played. Keigan Parker and Momo, in particular, were outstanding. The rest of the team had also played well but Keigan and Momo were the difference between the teams. We played Momo at right midfield so he was probably up against the strongest part of the Rangers team in Arthur Numan, Giovanni van Bronckhorst and Jorg Albertz, but he completely ripped them apart. These guys had all played at the highest level but they just couldn't handle Momo. His performance that day was probably his best in a St Johnstone jersey, he was unbelievable. That was a Rangers team who were streets ahead of everybody else but that day we produced a real performance and thoroughly deserved our win.

That was the good side but there were other times when I felt like I was banging my head off a brick wall with Momo. There was an incident where I lost it with him after an international break when he had gone back to France again. He came back a day late, not for the first time. I went right through him in front of all the players and then I pulled him into my office. I got the chief executive, Stewart Duff, in and we ended up disciplining Momo, fining him two weeks' wages. He then turned around and handed me a bag of presents for Liz and the kids. He bought me a pair of pyjamas with elephants on them, Liz a pair of shoes and toys for Gary and Nicky. We had a good relationship and I did feel a wee bit guilty that I had hammered him but I had to do it. He was pushing things too far. Other players argued that they would never have got away with what Momo did and that was another issue within the dressing room. I discussed things with the chairman Geoff Brown and right away he told me to get rid of Momo. A lot of the stuff with Momo I managed to keep under wraps, that was the way he was and you either put up with it or put him out. Don't get me wrong, he wasn't a bad lad, it was just his nature and the way he had been brought up. He didn't think he was doing anything wrong but at any club you have to have a code of conduct to keep everybody in order.

Momo kept pushing things to the limit and in the end Geoff told me just to free him, but I knew there was interest and I could get money for him. It is part of a manager's job to try and generate money for your club wherever you can. The good thing from Momo's point of view was that he always did well in the big games against the Old Firm. Martin O'Neill had not long taken over as Celtic manager. I ran into him a few times and he asked me my thoughts on Mo. I told Martin the truth, he was a good player but he could also be completely undisciplined. I gave him my views as to his strengths and where he let himself down. I was honest and up front. Martin came back to me and said, 'I will give you £500,000 for him,' but I refused because I felt we could get more than that. It was at a time when transfer markets were a bit more inflated and Martin came back and offered £750,000 to get the deal done, Geoff bit his hand off. This was a player he was ready to boot out the door for nothing and now he was getting £750,000 for him.

Momo went on to play in that strong Celtic team under Martin O'Neill, which was no mean feat. He was even on the bench when they got to the final of the UEFA Cup and I saw the game where he helped the Hoops win 2–0 against Liverpool at Anfield. You don't get to that level unless you can play and Momo, despite all his faults, certainly could.

To be fair to Geoff, he would tell me to get rid of a player but he would never actually force me to do it. He knew I was the manager and when it came to the football side of things the final decision was mine and mine alone. I didn't tell him how to do things in the boardroom and so he didn't tell me how my teams should be doing things out on the pitch. He had his opinions but the buck stopped with me. He paid me to manage his team and I always tried to do that to the best of my abilities.

Geoff was always quite grounded. He wanted St Johnstone to be the best they could be but he never had any great visions of grandeur. That was good because I don't think you have any divine right with a club the size of St Johnstone. Certainly if they are managed and run properly then they have a decent chance of being in there, especially when you compare them to the likes of Motherwell, Dunfermline, Partick Thistle and St Mirren. A lot of these clubs have yo-yoed over the years but St Johnstone, under Geoff, have always been pretty consistent. He always ran the club exceptionally well and within their means. He certainly saved the club, helped to build the new ground and I am pretty sure he has put quite a lot of his own money into the club. He has been one of the strongest chairman that Scottish football has seen for a long time. He really applies good business acumen along with a good understanding of football and he has been great for St Johnstone, there is no doubt about that. He has invested a lot of time and money into the football club but there was a stage when he tried to pull back a bit. He didn't want to put more of his own money into the club and I can completely understand why.

Nobody could doubt that Geoff is a St Johnstone fan but the game we clinched third spot in that first season, when we beat Dundee, he was away on holiday. The next season in the UEFA Cup he wasn't at the game in Monaco. These were two of the biggest games in the club's history and it really surprised me that he wasn't there. Maybe he had no option, but they were matches that the fans would have given their right arm to have been at.

26

DRUGS IN THAT BAR

I WILL never forget Monday, 24 December 2000. I went into McDiarmid Park like any other day, to continue with our preparations for our game against Rangers on Boxing Day. I was sitting in my office when there was a chap at my door and our physiotherapist, Nick Summersgill, walked in. He told me he had been out on Saturday with the players, who had been on their Christmas night out. He then revealed he had walked into the toilets in That Bar, a trendy pub in Perth, where he saw George O'Boyle and Kevin Thomas taking drugs. He told me they had a £20 note rolled up and were sniffing what he believed was cocaine. I just looked at him in total disbelief and said, 'What?' It took a bit of time for the reality of what Nick was telling me to sink in. I then asked Nick who else he had told. He revealed he had confronted the players in the toilet, but there wasn't much of a conversation and both George and Kevin had tried to laugh things off. He said he had also told the club doctor Alastair McCracken. That complicated the matter for me because Alastair was not only the doctor but also a director of St Johnstone. I was left in a real predicament, wondering how do I deal with this. If I am being honest, I didn't know what to do because no SFA badge or certificate could prepare you for something like that. I decided I needed to speak to the chairman, Geoff Brown. I phoned him and told him I needed to see him when he came into the club for his usual lunch-time visit.

I had to tell him because if it had leaked out then it was going to be a major issue for the club. I decided to keep everything close to my chest, so I went out and took training as normal and never said a word to any of the players, including Kevin or George, then I went in to see the chairman when I got back. I explained to him what had happened. Right away Geoff told me to sack them. He was adamant there was no place for drugs in football and as a family club we were unable to tolerate or condone such actions. I didn't disagree with that stance because footballers are role models and many young people look up to them. They had well and truly crossed the line.

Now looking back, with the help of hindsight, I wish Nick had never told Alastair because then I could have had the opportunity to deal with things differently. If he had left it in my hands then there would have been more chance I could have kept things in-house. I would have still put George and Kevin in their place. They had been stupid and had let their families, the club, me and more importantly themselves down, but I would seriously have considered keeping it between the three of us. I believe George and Kevin would have still learned their lesson without being dragged through such a public trial.

I don't know if taking another route would have been right but I would probably have gone that way, although morally telling the chairman was the right thing to do. It was his club, and it would be his team that was left tarnished. He would be the one left to pick up the pieces if it all came out.

After I had discussed things with Geoff I called George and Kevin into my office one at a time. They both initially denied they had taken drugs so I told them I knew they had and there was no point in trying to cover up. That was when they both admitted taking the drugs. George and Kevin both said it was a one-off and a mistake. Whether it was or not I will leave that for you to make up your own mind. In fairness to Kevin and George they had been out injured for long spells. They used that as part of their argument and had said they had taken drugs because they had been feeling down. They had both suffered serious knee injuries and had been going through a hard time in their bid to regain full fitness. The boys, to their credit, did hold their hands up and apologise to me after I pulled them in for those one-to-one meetings. I felt for them – but by that time it was too late.

I am told cocaine is a bit like alcohol. Within twenty-four hours it is out of your system and doesn't come up in a drugs test, so is unlikely to be flagged up in any random checks. There is no doubt George and Kevin had gone through some difficult and real low points, but at the same time I have also been in situations where I have been injured, dropped or even sacked, but I never once thought about using drugs. If you want to escape, for me, you can't beat a few pints of lager. You might have a sore head the next morning but you pick yourself up when reality kicks in and you get on with it. Maybe drugs are more apparent in the modern era but I just can't see the need or the attraction. If they needed somebody to talk to them then I would have easily gone out and had a few drinks with them, as I quite often did. These nights and evenings are all part of helping the team and squad to bond.

I just don't understand the fascination with drugs. It must have been the way I was brought up because I have never seen anybody take drugs, never mind deal in them. I must be totally naive because people tell me you can get drugs nearly anywhere. Certainly, if I found out any of my family were taking drugs then I would disown them, but you just don't know what is going on. Every parent probably says the same thing. Drugs were never an issue. I don't know much about them and that is the way I would like it to stay. I certainly would hate to see somebody close to me getting caught up in drugs.

George and Kevin were both informed they had been sacked via the club and their lawyers. I could no longer do anything, it was over my head. The players' union got involved and there were various legal fights and tribunals, as the players challenged the club's decision. It was horrendous as it dragged on for months and months. The various meetings and tribunals took up a lot of my time when I really should have been focusing all my efforts on the team and the results on the pitch. It was a massive unwanted distraction to the club.

I didn't speak to George or Kevin that much after they were sacked. They challenged their sackings through the SPL and independent tribunals and it wasn't pleasant sitting there, facing them and giving evidence against them. It was difficult, but in situations like that you can only tell the truth and that is what I did. I remember one of their lawyers asked me, 'Would you have wanted the player sacked if it had been Keigan Parker?' They were basically asking would the club have sacked one of their prized assets worth a lot of money? I knew what he was getting at but I couldn't answer it. I don't know what the club or board would have done, I was only the manager and I couldn't speak for them. The chairman said he would have treated every one of the players the same way, but I don't know. That is a question only Geoff Brown and his board could answer.

In football terms it was horrible, it just seemed so crazy. I also had more than a degree of sympathy with both players. I don't think either of them are bad people, but they got caught. I am not saying there is a massive drugs problem in Scottish football, but there is no way they are the only two players in the game who have taken drugs. I don't even know if they were the only two at St Johnstone. I just don't know. I read the riot act in the dressing room after the news came out and I threatened every player to within an inch of their lives that they would be taking the same route as Kevin and George if they were found to be taking or involved with drugs. It was the best deterrent we could lay down because George and Kevin basically lost their careers as a result of their actions. I think it stopped any other players potentially taking drugs. Whether it had the same effect at other clubs I am not so sure.

Kevin and George never kicked another ball for St Johnstone. There was never going to be any other outcome. They both tried to play on at lower levels but couldn't get themselves back up to the same levels as before. It was a sad way for their careers to peter out. I had played alongside George when he was at his peak at Dunfermline and he was a good player. Kevin also suffered a bad knee injury at Hearts, which curtailed him, otherwise he could have reached even higher levels than he did. I had him as a youngster at Tynecastle and there was no question Kevin had the potential to be a really top player. It was sad for me because I knew Kevin and all his family from our time together at Tynecastle. I also signed him from Morton because I felt he could still become a top-class player. Kevin and George both paid the ultimate price and I just hope that other professionals learn from the same pitfalls that cost these boys their top-flight careers.

The 2000–01 season ended up being an almighty struggle even though it had started with signs of promise. We famously beat Rangers and a few weeks later I knocked back the approach from Hearts and Chris Robinson. After that, though, the talk was more about off-the-field issues than football, as we finished disappointingly in tenth, in the now twelve-team league, although more importantly, still in the top flight.

27

SOME SAINTS AND SINNERS

AGGIE MOFFAT is probably the most famous tea lady Scottish football has ever seen. She was famed for taking Graeme Souness to task when he was manager of Rangers. Aggie was 'Mrs St Johnstone'. She did just about everything at the club from tea to kit lady. I got on really well with her and she was a good source of information for me. She wouldn't tell on players but she would give me an idea of things I should know. Aggie was a good person to have about the place.

She would do the strips for all matches although she didn't go to the away games. She packed all the hampers and got them ready and loaded on to the team bus.

Jocky Peebles was the bag man at reserve games and used to help out at the club on match days. He is still at the club now. I tried to make the club a bit more professional and asked, 'Why do we not get a full-time kitman?' I asked if Jocky could do it as when it came to away games we didn't have anybody to sort the kit out. Normally it would be left to Billy Kirkwood or some of the staff and players to do it. I went to the board to ask about employing Jocky, but they said they didn't have the money. Every top team has a full-time kitman now but back then the St Johnstone board said no. The directors gave me two reasons for knocking me back – it would upset Aggie and they didn't

have the money for another full-time wage. I know for a fact
Aggie wouldn't have bothered if we told her why we were
taking somebody else in. I also told them if they were that bothered about the money then they could take it off my wages, but
they wouldn't do that either. Everybody at St Johnstone had to
muck in and do whatever was asked. There is nothing wrong
with that because that was what I had been used to at Hearts,
but I was just trying to push the club forward and make it that
bit more professional, but it wasn't to be.

There were times when I had to keep some of my own players
on the straight and narrow. The main one was Keigan Parker.
He was a great young player, who lived locally to me in Bathgate.
At times he was Jack the Lad. I knew him inside out and I could
tell right away if he was trying to fob me off with wee white
lies, like whether he had been drinking or not. It was good he
lived nearby because it meant I could keep a close eye on him.
There was no escape for him, which was just as well because
Keigan used to have an eye for the ladies. I remember he had
been trying it on with a girl, but she had quite a big boyfriend
who came looking for Keigan one Christmas Day. He phoned
me in a total panic and said he didn't know what to do. I told
him he'd better get his stuff and come and stay at our house
because I needed him fit and in one piece for our Boxing Day
fixture. It meant an extra bed being filled, but at least Keigan
had the good grace to let us get our Christmas dinner out of the
way before he arrived.

Keigan wasn't much older than my boys, Gary and Nicky,
and was like one of the family at times. He got a bit of stick
from some of the boys at the club because we were quite close
but it never really bothered him. He was also responsible for
almost maiming Nicky. The boys used to have a quad bike and
over the years they had battered it about, leaving a bit of rough

metal flapping at the front. Keigan was on it when he skidded on some stones, flew into Nicky and caught him right on the knee. There was blood pouring everywhere and I got the fright of my life when I saw his leg. His skin was flapping and there was a gaping hole in his knee. Liz nearly fainted when she saw the mess of it. I went and got a towel but within minutes it had turned red. We got Nicky into the car and raced up to St John's Hospital in Livingston. Keigan just stood there in a state of shock. He had got the fright of his life, fearing what he had done. I was battering up to the hospital when I saw Keigan driving behind us in his car. Nicky was lying across his mum, but when he heard Keigan was there he was up waving and shouting at him. Keigan was one of his heroes even though he was never away from the house. We managed to get Nicky to the hospital and stitched up and he still has a scar as a reminder of that ill-fated day. Nicky now tells all the girls when he is out that it was a shark bite and not that it was down to Keigan's handiwork.

Keigan was one of the younger members of my squad while at the opposite end of the spectrum was the vastly-experienced Alan Main. He was a great goalkeeper and a tremendous servant to St Johnstone. Jim Weir was the club captain but had been out for a long time with an Achilles injury and so Alan had the armband for long spells. He was a player that led by example, was really consistent and rarely made a mistake. Having a goalkeeper of Alan's class inspired confidence in the defence and was worth a good few points a season. He broke into the Scotland set-up and was unfortunate that the country had so many top goalkeepers at that time, otherwise he would have won a lot of caps.

Alan was a strong character. Not long before I left he made it clear he wasn't happy about various issues, although he was still my No. 1. Alan always had ambitions to go and play else-where, and there is absolutely nothing wrong with that.

Three weeks before I got sacked, Alan came to me and said, 'I want to move.' I asked him why and he said things were just not right and he wanted to go. He had put his transfer request in writing but I asked him if he would keep it and give it another few weeks because he might be dealing with another manager by then. I knew by our results I was under pressure and the axe could fall at any point. I asked him if he would hold off but he didn't. He went to the chief executive Stewart Duff and handed it to him. I was really disappointed with his timing, not because he wanted to go, but I felt he did it at a time when we needed everyone to stick together and show their unity.

I have seen Alan many times since and the good times always outweigh the bad. When I think of Alan I always recall that save against Dundee that helped us to clinch third spot. That showed his quality as one of the best goalkeepers that St Johnstone has ever had.

Alan was already at the club before I took over, though I brought in a few of my own signings, including a number of foreign imports. I first went to watch Tommy Lovenkrands, I liked him as a player and was able to do a quick deal to sign him from AB Copenhagen in 2000. I would have loved to have signed his brother, Peter Lovenkrands, as well. We had a wee go but it was never going to happen. I think it was well known within football that Peter was destined for bigger things and it turned out to be the case when he signed for Rangers a couple of weeks later.

Tommy was a big confidence player, at times he would be incredible and at other times he would have no belief in himself and do daft things like fall over the ball. He could have achieved a bit more if he'd had more confidence in himself. He probably didn't play the best football of his career at St Johnstone, although nobody could ever accuse him of not giving 100 percent. There are very few people I can look back at in my career and say they didn't give me everything. That is all you can ask from anybody in football or life.

28

SACKED SANDY

THE END for me at St Johnstone came down to a combination of factors. There was the George O'Boyle and Kevin Thomas issue and the fact that some of my new signings had failed to gel the way I had hoped. There was also a growing expectation at the club and that was down to how successful we had been in finishing third and then fifth before we slipped down to tenth. Another major issue was the introduction of the Bosman Ruling and the damage it did to clubs like St Johnstone. We just couldn't compete financially with most of our SPL rivals.

I was really disappointed when I was shown the door because I firmly believed that I would have turned things around. I knew we were struggling but I still felt in control of the situation. I accept we are in a results-based business and we hadn't got enough points on the board but I still had faith in my team and my players that we would turn the corner. I might have got more time if the chairman Geoff Brown had been more hands on. At that point he was dealing with the far more pressing matters of his health as he battled prostate cancer, so my predicament and that of his club, understandably, weren't at the forefront of his mind. Also, Motherwell were down beside us at the foot of the table and they sacked their manager, Billy Davies. I am sure that would also have come into the thinking of the St Johnstone directors when it came to showing me the door.

I knew there was a possibility I could be fired because results weren't what they should have been. I was aware of mutterings of discontent from the boardroom. There was a director at the club, Douglas McIntyre, who I didn't have any time for. You hear a lot of the tittle-tattle that goes on around a football club and he had apparently been regularly slaughtering the team and the players from the directors' box. I had found out about it so I decided to go to the chairman because the boardroom was under his jurisdiction. I went to Geoff and said we are a team and we have to stick together, we can't have our own directors slaughtering the players. I expected Geoff to take control of the situation, but he completely opted out. He told me if I wasn't happy then I should go and see Douglas.

I felt Geoff should have dealt with it but he didn't and so I decided to take the bull by the horns. I took him into my office and confronted him. He confirmed he had been critical of some of the team so I gave him what for and told him that the players and I would appreciate if he could get behind us rather than harangue us all the time, although it was in a much more industrial manner. Douglas just sat there. His face was beetroot red and he never said a word, didn't even stand up and defend himself or challenge me for the way I had taken him to task. I would have thought more of him if he had been critical to my face or to the players but he wasn't. Yes, of course people have the right to criticise but in my view, club directors should either offer constructive criticism or support and puting the knife in helps no one. When I was sacked I am in absolutely no doubt what side of the fence he would have been on and it wasn't mine.

My last game was a 4–0 loss against Hibs. It was ironic because I had just travelled halfway around the world before the game to watch a couple of potential signings in action. I jetted out to see the Ecuadorian international midfielders Edison Mendez and Wellington Sanchez play against Argentina in the Copa America. I had met an agent in New York and flew out with him. Ulises de la Cruz, who went on to star for Hibs, played in the game but my men didn't show up the way I had hoped and I decided not to pursue my interest. It was an awful long way to go for nothing, a waste of time and my return home also ended up being a total nightmare. I got to the airport in the Ecuadorian capital of Quito but they had over-booked the flight and I couldn't get back. I had to fly to Columbia, then wait for hours in Bogotá before I flew back to Paris. I finally made it to Glasgow just in time for the game against Hibs. The result and our performance didn't exactly help my mood either.

I went in and took training on the Monday and waited at the ground to watch the reserve team. Stewart Duff and the vice chairman Ian Dewar then called me in and told me, 'It's bad news.' I knew what was happening and there wasn't much of a conversation. I agreed I would come back up to Perth the next day for the press conference. They could have their say and I could have mine and I could also say my goodbyes to the players and staff. It was difficult because I was disappointed with how things had ended and so were the rest of the staff, but the bottom line was I had been sacked and that was it. I walked out and that was the end of my time at St Johnstone.

I still don't know how much say or influence Geoff Brown had in the decision but a few days after I had been sacked he left an answer-phone message. He said something along the lines of, 'Sandy, I am really sorry with what has happened and I hope things are okay?' The first thing I did after that was to go up to visit him at Murrayfield Hospital. I think he got the fright of his life when he saw me coming up to his bed. He thought I was going to give him what for but that was never going to be the case. I appreciated Geoff giving me the opportunity and I just wanted to thank him for all his support. I think he was quite pleased to see me and I don't think we mentioned football once. We spoke more about how he was getting on health-wise and family matters than anything to with what had happened. Geoff beating cancer was far more important than me losing my job as a football manager. Geoff, to be fair, paid up my contract and I got every penny I was due.

My mum also died that same year to really compound my misery. She was seventy years of age and died of lung cancer. She had smoked all her days but it didn't really affect her too much until that final year. The one thing about my mum, she had always been there for me to help me and support me throughout my life, through thick and thin, when the kids were born or when my first marriage broke down. I owed her a lot and her death hit the family and me hard. It was a difficult period for us all.

Thankfully for Geoff and St Johnstone he recovered from his cancer fight and everything is fine now. I have come across Geoff a few times at games and he always says hello but we have never had any in-depth conversations or discussions. Geoff is always polite and courteous but can't get away quick enough.

I went for the Kilmarnock job after I left St Johnstone, and I was told that a couple of the directors wanted to appoint me but another one had got a bad reference from St Johnstone. If that was the case then I would be very disappointed.

I think Geoff blames me for the club getting relegated. He has his opinions why things went wrong and I have mine. I think it is fair to say it is something we will never agree on. I had to find replacements and bring in players of similar quality to John O'Neil and John McQuillan on free transfers, and that was near impossible. To get similar quality was going to cost money, money he wasn't willing to invest. I decided to go down the road of experience and brought in the former Scotland striker Darren Jackson and Benito Kemble, the Dutch central defender, from Motherwell. Geoff was critical of my signing policy but my argument to that is if you have the lowest wage budget in the league, which I had, then you are always going to get the last pick of players. I am not absolving myself of the blame because maybe I didn't network as much as I should have. I should have got more out of the people and contacts I have down in England. I also should have tried some unknown players from down south rather than going down the route of older players, who were tried and trusted. That proved to be my downfall because the legs of Darren, Benito and some of the older players had started to go.

Geoff, maybe, has an argument on that front, but it was also at a time he had pulled away from the club. He had his health problems and wasn't prepared to put in the extra financial backing, but I have never been one to complain about budgets. Anywhere I have worked I have operated within a budget and I know the club's survival is more important than anything else.

The hardest part of managing is signing the right players. I can accept the criticism that some of my signings didn't set the heather alight, but I also had my fair share of successes as well. Momo Sylla and Paul Hartley were good signings for St Johnstone. Graeme Jones I would class as another success. He was similar in style to myself and if I had stayed on at the club I am in no doubt he could have been central to any future success but these things happen as a football manager.

I also bought Peter MacDonald from Rangers. He was at the club a long time and was a big success at McDiarmid Park. Had it not been for injury he would have scored a lot more goals.

John-Paul McBride did struggle while Craig Russell tried his heart out and had a great attitude but it just didn't happen for them. You also have to consider the bigger picture. When a trialist wants to come to Scotland or an agent is trying to bring a player across then they start at the high end, Rangers and Celtic, and then go to the Hearts, Hibs, Aberdeen or Dundee United. St Johnstone were always last because we were paying the least amount of money. Most players are mercenaries and who can blame them? If they are coming to Scotland they aren't going to sign for us because they are St Johnstone fans – they are going to go where the money is. That is a simple fact. I took a bit of stick over my transfer dealings but I am certain St Johnstone ended up in profit from my time there, through the sale of players, cup runs, Europe and our final league positions.

I have a great affiliation with my former clubs and a bond, but that has never really been the case for me and St Johnstone. I know the St Johnstone team who finished third in the league and got to the cup final had a reunion a few years ago but I was never invited. My time at St Johnstone was a perfect example of the way football is. I had really good spells where it couldn't really have gone any better, unless we had won a cup. We also had difficult spells where it was hard, like the introduction of the Bosman Ruling, the drugs situation and the chairman being ill. That is life and you just have to play the hand you are dealt.

Geoff announced he was stepping down as chairman of St Johnstone late in 2011 after he appointed Steve Lomas as his new manager. It is fair to say St Johnstone and the people of Perth owe him a lot for what he has given to the football club and the city. We had our ups and downs but Geoff always put the interests of St Johnstone before anything else. The club achieved a lot under him and Scottish football will be a lot poorer without a character and person like Geoff Brown.

29

DANNY WILSON AND CO.

AFTER I left St Johnstone in 2001 I suddenly found myself with time on my hands. Suddenly I didn't have football going round my head all the time. Anyone who has been involved in football and in particular the management side of the game knows you can never switch off, it is a twenty-four/seven job. There is no escape. Unfortunately, that means the people who suffer most are the people closest to you – your family. You don't always give them the time and attention you should. I tried to set time aside for the family but you always knew your phone could go at any time, whether it be a chairman, a player, agent, journalist or somebody phoning to ask about a player.

So, although being out of a job was a major setback it at least gave me a bit more time to spend with Liz, Gary, Nicky and Suzi. It was good to do the everyday things that a dad and a husband take for granted. I always tried to go and watch Gary and Nicky play football whenever I could, but sometimes it was hard, especially if St Johnstone had a game on a Sunday afternoon, away from home. Gary loved to play football and gave it his all, but it is fair to say his talents lay elsewhere. He is now forging a career for himself in the Royal Navy. Suzi qualified as a primary teacher but is now doing well in the police. It gives me just as much pride seeing Gary and Suzi doing well in their respective jobs as it does seeing Nicky play professional football. I am proud of every one of my kids, they have all done themselves and their parents proud.

Nicky was the only one who decided to follow in his dad's footsteps. He kicked off by playing for Balbardie Primary School in Bathgate and then showed a bit of talent playing with Bathgate Rose and Armadale. Gary Brown, who had been a scout for me at Hearts, Hamilton and St Johnstone, then got him a trial with the Livingston-based Murieston United Boys Club. Murieston is more of a community football club. They have a whole host of age groups, from under-8s and 9s right up to amateur teams. They have a great set-up and the guys there dedicate a lot of time and hard work to keep the club going.

Nicky went there and did well. He started off playing seven-a-side football and I would go and see Nicky and his Murieston team whenever I could. Nicky was a good player and I thought he had a chance to maybe make a name for himself in the professional game. It helped that Nicky's Murieston team had some exceptional talent. There was a young, budding Danny Wilson, Darren Cole and Rhys McCabe, who all ended up at Rangers, and the Jacobs triplets, Devon, Sheldon and Kyle. All three Jacobs brothers also went on to play for Livingston, along with the goalkeeper Darren Jamieson.

I started to go to the games solely as a supportive parent although I could see they had some exceptional young talent. John Mochan, whose son, Kevin, also played for the team, and Dave Jacobs, the triplets' father, ran that Murieston team. Kevin remains one of Nicky's best pals and is almost like my third son because he is never away from our house. He pretty much lives with us most of the time, especially at the weekend, although I have never got round to charging him rent, yet.

John and Dave asked me if I could help them and maybe take a couple of training sessions. I was at a loose end and I felt why not give something back. The boys enjoyed the training sessions and I have to admit I got a buzz working with the kids. The next thing I knew Dave and John had roped me in to taking the team. Their excuse was that I was an experienced manager while they were better organising things behind the scenes, like sorting out the training gear and planning the travel arrangements. They set me up big-time but I was more than happy to help, especially as we had such a good group of boys, on and off the pitch. To be fair to John and Dave they certainly had an eye for a player and had put a really good bunch of players together with that Murieston squad.

I took the team and we never looked back. I can certainly claim very little of the credit because the kids were all extremely talented and the foundations had already been put in place by John and Dave. After my first season we moved up to eleven-a-side and started playing in the East of Scotland league, which was from under-11s. We played against a lot more of the established and bigger teams from Edinburgh, like Hutchison Vale and Tynecastle Boys Club. All these sides were able to call on the catchment of the capital. These teams used to turn up at the matches with their tracksuits and training kits, probably better turned out than a lot of the senior sides. Murieston were the exact opposite. We were rag-tag and bobtail with the boys all turning up in their own tracksuits and clothes. But when our boys stepped on to the pitch they were a cut above.

From under-11s to under-13s we won three leagues in a row without losing a game. It was some achievement. We beat everybody. At times it wasn't ideal because in some matches we were winning matches 8–0 and 9–0. There was a bit of a gulf between us and some of the teams. It wasn't the players' faults, they could only beat what was put in front of them but at times the games were a bit of a mismatch, although it was a lot closer when we played some of the bigger teams. I tried to keep our players on their toes by setting them little challenges, like if our goalkeeper let in a goal then all the boys would have to do some extra running in the next training session. I never actually made them do the extra running but the threat kept them on their toes and focused.

There were other things the boys had to cope with, especially when we went to more hostile environments, like when we played some of the local teams in Leith. It could be a pretty intimidating experience for the boys with all the parents and their supporters shouting and screaming at the kids. Any youth coach will tell you that one of the biggest problems at that level of football is interference from parents. The one rule I had at Murieston was that the parents could come to the game but I didn't want them shouting from the sidelines and getting involved in what I was trying to do with the team. To be fair to every parent they stuck by those rules although it wasn't always the case with some of the opposing teams we faced.

Early on some of the kids were a bit wary of the more hostile environments but once we got them organised and got them to do the right things they were fine and they let their football do the talking.

The team got a lot of good press, especially in the *Edinburgh Evening News*. We upset a lot of the more established teams with our success because we were stealing some of the limelight away from them. The likes of Hutchie Vale were probably our closest challengers but they just couldn't beat us.

Our captain was Kyle Jacobs. He was an out-and-out winner and he had a real determination not to lose. Kyle ran the midfield and Nicky played alongside him or as a striker. Nicky chipped in with a few goals as did Rhys McCabe, while Darren Cole and Danny Wilson played at the back. I will never forget Danny in those early years, he was as blind as a bat and it was before he could get contact lenses, so he had to wear these protective sports glasses, which were probably an earlier version of what the legendary Dutch star Edgar Davids used to wear. He needed to wear his glasses and I always put it down to his dad, John, who had a short spell as a goalkeeper with Celtic. John and his wife, Nicki, used to come to all the games as did Granddad and Grandma Wilson. That was good because Grandma Wilson always ensured the Murieston sideline had a never-ending supply of sweets.

Danny was a very tall kid for age although he was also very skinny. He wasn't the most aggressive, let me put it that way. He might not have looked like a budding Scotland international at first glance but as soon as he took to the field you could see he was special. Danny could read the game, he had a great left foot and his attitude was also excellent. He did, however, need to be toughened up. I have to hold my hands up and admit that maybe early on I roughed up Danny a bit on the training field, to try and toughen him up. It wasn't quite bullying, although I knew he would have a real chance if he became a bit more physical. The good thing was that I had his dad's 100 percent backing. I think it worked and Danny did develop more of a physical presence. Danny was also an intelligent kid. He excelled at school and could have quite easily gone to university had he not turned professional.

It is not a surprise to me that Danny has got to the level he has, winning a move to a big Premier League team like Liverpool and also becoming a full Scotland international. Physically he was a man. He had the height, he also had a real natural intelligence to read the game and he is a very good user of the ball, with either foot. I can still see areas of his game where he needs to improve but Danny would be the first to admit that himself. Danny was also helped by the fact he is very grounded and is from a good family. As with all the kids, what Danny has achieved in the game is down to himself, I only gave them all a bit of direction and more awareness of the game. After that it was up to them to take the step forward and practise every aspect of their play. Danny did that and as a result he has got to the top level.

The youth coaches at Ibrox and the former Rangers manager Walter Smith also have to take a lot of credit for helping Danny along the way. He couldn't have got a better manager to work under than Walter. As a boss he would never put players into situations if he didn't think they could handle it. The fact Walter threw Danny into the Champions League showed just what he thought of him as a player and a person. He obviously felt Danny was up to playing at that level and Danny went out and proved Walter was right to have faith in him. Even before he had kicked a ball for Rangers he had a decent reputation. The likes of Tottenham Hotspur and Blackburn Rovers were both keen to get a hold of him but thankfully for Rangers they managed to fend other clubs off. They got him into their first team and gave him some decent exposure before they sold him for a decent fee to Liverpool. I think that is only right because Rangers had put so much time and work into Danny's development.

Ironically, if circumstances had been different then Danny would have ended up at Livingston rather than in the youth ranks of Murray Park. Murieston had a good reputation and quite a lot of clubs, like Aberdeen, Hearts, Hibs and Falkirk, were all interested in signing some of the boys. I went across to speak to Jim Leishman, who was in charge of Livingston at the time, to discuss the possibility of them taking the boys on back in 2003. They wanted to sign some of the players but I wanted them to take on the whole team and play under the name of Livingston FC. I was also keen to keep working with the boys and the team. I had spoken to the boys and their parents and they had said that if they were going to go to Livingston then they wanted me to come as well. Livingston, in the end, decided they didn't want that or maybe it was just me they didn't want – I don't know. That decision, I am sure, will now haunt them even though the Jacob triplets and Darren Jamieson later went on to play for them. They could have had the whole team, including Danny Wilson, but they had other ideas.

I took the boys down to Everton to play a game against their youth team and to have a look around the set-up at Goodison Park. I know Davie Moyes well, I had played against him many times and we did our UEFA Pro-Licence together. He was the manager at Everton and so I phoned him to arrange the trip and we hired a bus and headed for Merseyside, with a few family and friends tagging on. For some of the boys it was a new experience because some had never been out of Scotland. To be fair the boys weren't fazed because even against a top English side they showed up well. They beat a young Everton side 2–1. That led to Everton expressing an interest in a few of the boys but they were only thirteen or fourteen at the time, they were still very young and Liverpool was just too far away for them to go. Maybe if it had happened a couple of years later it might have been different, but I knew then some of that team were really going to go places.

I spoke to the local Rangers scout, Robin Gibson, and he asked if he could take some of the kids into Murray Park. I didn't think it was fair to hold the boys back. Kyle Jacobs, Danny and Nicky were the three boys they wanted. They went in and did well in training with Rangers, I organised a game between Murieston and the Rangers youth team. We went into Murray Park and beat that Rangers team 7–3. After that they ended up taking eight boys in to train, including Rhys McCabe. That was great although the only problem was trying to get the kids from Livingston to Murray Park for training twice a week. But it is something that parents the length and breadth of the country have to put up with on a weekly basis.

It was at Murray Park that I came across my former Rangers manager, John Greig, when I took the boys in for training. John was always good value and would laugh and joke and say, 'I can't believe I paid all that money for you.' I still got on really well with him and he was always great with all the young boys. He made a real effort to get to know them and all their parents.

Nicky was quite small for his age. John said to Liz one night, 'What is the wee man doing with Sandy's shorts on?' I know Nicky thought the world of him through that short time they had at Murray Park and he really appreciated working with one of the true legends of the Scottish game. Nicky's problem at Rangers was, like myself, he was quite small for his age. Nicky suffered badly with growing pains, also like I had at his age. I had had Osgood Schlatters disease, which was growing pains in my knees, while Nicky had Sever's disease, which is growing pains around the ankles. He suffered a lot with that and it really affected him. I experienced it first-hand and I had also seen the impact it had on other young players, like Gary Locke when I had taken the youths at Hearts.

Stephen Wright was in charge of that Rangers youth team. When they got to around under-15 level he let quite a few of the players go and Nicky was one of them. He felt Nicky was too small and just not good enough. I had watched a lot of their games and I know I am Nicky's dad and people might think I am biased but I felt he was good enough to be kept on. I didn't even discuss things with Wright when we were told Nicky was being released. I didn't think it was worth the bother because he didn't really fancy him as a player. I knew after Nicky got over his growing problems he would kick on. It would have been easy for us to say to Nicky, 'It hasn't worked out so why don't you look at another career?' I just felt he had too much natural ability to throw it all away. He maybe wasn't going to make it at Rangers but he was definitely good enough to play professionally.

As for a lot of the other Murieston boys, they have gone on to make a name for themselves in the lower leagues. Darren Cole and Rhys McCabe have already made top-team appearances for Rangers and look to have bright futures ahead of them. Hopefully one or two can also still get to the level Danny Wilson has got to because they definitely have the ability. Watching all the boys make their way at different levels gives me enormous satisfaction even if I might have complained at times when after a heavy Saturday night I was forced to get up at 8.30 on a Sunday morning for the games. That was my only bugbear. When you saw them play and the determination and enthusiasm they showed it started to rub off on me because they were so infectious. We had a good bond and enjoyed what we were doing, even on a wet Tuesday night on public pitches. They really were a great bunch of boys and I am not just saying that, the pluses definitely outweighed the minuses.

That Murieston team also shows there is still a lot of ability in this country. I firmly believe there is a lot of exceptional young, talent in Scotland. Even when I was at Aberdeen there were a lot of good prospects coming through. For me, the talent is definitely out there and it is up to the people in the game to make sure those players are spotted and developed properly. I have massive fears about the game financially but I don't have any worries that Scotland will run out of natural talent.

I was first-team coach at Aberdeen when Nicky was released by Rangers. I spoke to Lenny Taylor, who was in charge of the Pittodrie youth set-up, about him. He had seen Nicky play at Rangers, so when I explained the circumstances, right away Lenny said, 'That is fine, bring him to us.' He finished his schooling and at sixteen he signed professional forms with Aberdeen. I left Nicky to his own devices at Aberdeen as I didn't want any accusations of nepotism. I was with the first team and I didn't have a lot of dealings with Nicky. I watched from a distance as the young boys, like Peter Pawlett, Ryan Jack and Michael Paton, came through the ranks. That was good because everyone at Pittodrie knows how important it is to produce home-grown players.

Nicky had three good years at Pittodrie and made the bench a couple of times, so that showed he wasn't too far away from things. Jimmy Calderwood also gave him a couple of new contracts and I can honestly say I didn't know anything about them. Anyone who knows Jimmy knows he is the ultimate professional, he won't do you any favours and if you don't do things properly then you would be out on your ear. Maybe in different circumstances Nicky might still have been at Pittodrie.

He was eventually released after Mark McGhee replaced Jimmy Calderwood as manager. Nicky had been on loan at Peterhead but the director of football Willie Miller and McGhee decided he wasn't going to be kept on. Nicky went back to Peterhead for a short spell and is now at Queen of the South and doing well in the First Division.

Suzi, Gary and Nicky have all made me proud. They have done exceptionally well in their respective careers. Susan, or Suzi as she likes to be known, is now in the police and she is flourishing there. She is really happy with the way things have panned out and is happy in her life.

Gary always wanted to become a professional footballer but he was never quite good enough. He tried hard but was a wee bit short of what was required. Gary decided to go down a different route. He has always had a love of military aircraft, from Harriers to the frontline jets. He could tell you anything about them and decided to pursue a career in that field. After a very strict selection procedure he joined the Royal Navy as a sub-lieutenant officer with their Air Arm. He has been there for a couple of years and is now in the process of learning to fly.

Liz, Suzi, Nicky and I were all down in Dartmouth for Gary's passing out parade and it was a day that gave us all a lot of pride. He has a marvellous career in front of him. He now plays for the Royal Navy's football team and claims he is their best player – but whether that is true or not, I don't know.

30

DUNFERMLINE – ON A PAR WITH THE TWO JIMMYS

I HAD been working with the BBC full-time when I took a phone call from Jimmy Calderwood in the summer of 2003, offering me a coaching role under him and Jimmy Nicholl at Dunfermline Athletic. He wanted me to take the reserves and help with the first team. I didn't know Jimmy until he came back from Holland, I then came across him when my St Johnstone sides had clashed with Dunfermline. We got on well and would talk quite a bit when we met up at games. We built up a decent rapport from the off, so when he offered me the job I went and had a chat with him and was delighted to take up the position, and as I was still able to combine my television and radio commitments, it worked out well.

The more the season went on the more I got involved with the first-team games and training. The two Jimmys and I had a good working relationship and I also enjoyed working with the Dunfermline players, especially the strikers Stevie Crawford and Craig Brewster. We had some excellent players, like Barry Nicholson, Scott Wilson, Scott Thomson and Andrius Skerla, along with the Young brothers, Derek and Darren, who had come from Aberdeen. Another young striker who really caught my eye was Billy Mehmet. He is one of the best young finishers I have seen and has gone on to carve out a half-decent career.

Things went well on the park although off it things weren't as rosy. Financially, the club struggled and all the players and staff had to take wage cuts. We all had to take ten percent cuts in our salary and all bonuses were scrapped. There were cutbacks across the board from the office to the playing staff. It was a shame because there were lots of good people behind the scenes at Dunfermline, some who lost their jobs. There was John Ritchie, who was head of the youth set-up, and Mo Hutton, the kitman, who I will always remember for his dancing exploits on our trips to Majorca. Another was Scott Thomson, who is now at Hibs and is probably one of the hardest-working goal-keeping coaches around. People like that were part of the backroom staff and helped make Dunfermline a really enjoyable place to work.

It was a tough time, financially, but it was to everyone's credit that we finished the season so well, making the top six and in the Scottish Cup final. We faced Celtic at Hampden in Henrik Larsson's final farewell. There was only ever going to be one person grabbing the headlines that day and it wasn't going to be anyone in black and white. We took a shock lead through Skerla but lost 3–1, with Mr Larsson netting a double. Larsson was phenomenal at Celtic, most things he touched ended up in the back of the opposition's net. He is one of the best players Scottish football has seen in recent years.

At the end of that season we went out to Majorca, where Jimmy Calderwood owns a house in Santa Ponsa. We were in Spain when Aberdeen asked for permission to speak to Jimmy. The Dunfermline chairman John Yorkston tried desperately to keep him at East End Park, but, in the end, Jimmy decided he wanted to go to Aberdeen and agreed a deal to move to Pittodrie. Jimmy Nicholl went with him as his No. 2. They were also keen to take me but the timing wasn't right for me.

I spoke to the Dunfermline chairman John Yorkston about the possibility of replacing Jimmy as manager. We had a discussion and then I had to wait for the Dunfermline board to go through the selection process, although, if I am being honest, I never really thought I was going to get the job. I went away on holiday to St Lucia when my phone went and it was the director of football and my old Dunfermline boss, Jim Leishman, to tell me that I wasn't getting it. Dunfermline had decided to go with Davie Hay, which was fine, but then he told me that my services as a coach were no longer required. I knew that was going to happen, as I was working without a contract and every new manager wants to work with their own staff.

I was still a little bit devilish with Jim Leishman and said, 'That is fine, I will come and see you when I get back to find out the reason as to why I am being sacked.'

I have known Jim for a long time and so I went back to East End Park to see him. I still laugh to this day because I am still waiting for Jim to give me a reason. He kept telling me that he didn't know why I had been sacked and I should still be at the club. It was a bit cruel but I just wanted to see how Jim would react.

After I left Dunfermline I went on to manage Berwick Rangers for six or seven months until near the end of the 2004–05 season before deciding to join up with Jimmy Calderwood at Aberdeen again. I really enjoyed working with the Berwick chairman, Robert Wilson, the secretary, Dennis McCleary, and all the people at the club, and I had a brilliant, short spell there.

The thing that got me more than anything was the mentality of the players at Berwick. I had been used to working with full-time players but these boys, like Ian Little, Mark Cowan, were all part-time, and their attitudes were amazing. There were also a few boys who had been youngsters at Hearts, like Gary

O'Connor, David Murie, Grant McNichol and Robbie Horn, so it was good to work with them again. They had day jobs but when you got to training you would ask them to run and they would ask you how far and for how long. It was in complete contrast to a lot of the full-time players who would moan their faces off if you asked some of them to come back and do some extra work in the afternoon. The attitude of the part-time boys at Berwick was first class and I couldn't have asked for any more from them.

31

THE BLUES BROTHERS

A LOT was made about the fact that Jimmy Calderwood was a Rangers fan and both Jimmy Nicholl and I had spells at Ibrox as players. Some people dubbed us 'The Blues Brothers'. It was a laugh and a joke to a lot of people, but it didn't matter if we were playing Rangers or Atletico Madrid, all three of us were desperate to win, regardless of whether we were at Dunfermline, Aberdeen or Kilmarnock. We wanted to win every game and treated every match the same way. We would all have kicked our grannies if it guaranteed us the three points.

All three of us are really close and we had lots of nights out together, either the three of us or with our wives. We all get on really well and love to go out for a drink and to have a laugh and a joke. Normally, Jimmy Nicholl is at the centre of everything, being the daft Irishman he is. We have great times. Yes, we enjoy the social side of things but never let it get in the way of the football. When it came to football there was nobody more professional than the three of us.

We always tried to create a good atmosphere in our dressing rooms and out on the training pitch. We knew by doing that we would get the best out of the players. Jimmy Nicholl was the master of that with his on-going cons. I don't know how many players he has stitched up through the years. Darren Mackie was one of the unlucky ones who Jimmy did up like a kipper when we were at Aberdeen. Darren, as you know, is no slouch and was one of the quickest players at Pittodrie. Jimmy walked up to Darren and said, 'I will race you from the halfway line to the eighteen yards box for a fiver.' Darren just looked at him and laughed. Jimmy kept at him and Darren eventually joked, 'You're an old man, you have no chance.' Jimmy refused to take no for an answer and then said, 'If you are so confident I will race you for a fiver.' Darren eventually relented and agreed to the race. I was the starter and shouted go. They both set off, one a lot quicker than the other, Darren, obviously, beat him by a country mile. I think he had been in, showered and changed and back out again before Jimmy had even finished. Darren was waiting at the finishing line for Jimmy and said to him, 'That's a fiver you owe me.' Jimmy quick as a flash, replied, 'No, you owe me a fiver. I didn't say I'd beat you, I just said I would race you!' Let's put it this way Darren isn't the only one who has been stung by that trick.

He was also fond of another trick, which he used a few times with some of the young boys at Dunfermline. He would get an empty cup and would say, 'I bet you I can run round this park before you drink this cup of water.' The young trainee answered, 'Without cutting the corners? If you don't then I will take you up on that bet.' Jimmy replied, 'Yes', and then shouted to the kitman, Mo Hutton, to stick on the kettle for the boy. Jimmy ran round the park and came back and took the boy's money before the kettle had even finished boiling! Jimmy's daft wee pranks and stunts kept everyone on their toes.

There were times when the players would try to get their revenge, especially when we were at Aberdeen. They used to leave cups of water over the doors so when somebody walked in they would get soaked. Things like that go on at every club.

These wee things are good for lifting morale and the spirit. It can be a little bit childish at times but can be good if done at the right time.

When you are a boss and it comes to picking your backroom staff people normally tend to shy away from former managers. The concern is that if things go wrong then they could end up taking your job, but Jimmy Calderwood never worried about that, even though Jimmy Nicholl and I had been successful managers in our own right. Jimmy showed enormous belief in himself, and rightly so, that he wasn't frightened or intimated by our presence and believed we could all bring something to the table. He was willing to take what we could offer and use it to his benefit. The longer we worked together the more the belief and bond grew between us. Jimmy Calderwood didn't have any worries because he knew both Jimmy Nicholl and I were behind him 100 percent. Neither of us would have stabbed him in the back and gone looking for his job.

I have certainly learned a lot from working with Jimmy Calderwood, from coaching to management. Jimmy picked up a lot of valuable knowledge in Holland, which enhanced our training sessions and the organisation of our teams. He brought a different approach from his time with Willem II and NEC Nijmegen and that along with the stuff I have picked up in my own career has helped to make me a better coach and manager.

Jimmy is also very open and gave both Jimmy and myself our place. We would have a lot of meetings. If things were going well then we would try and cement things and when things weren't going so well we would look at ways to turn things around. Jimmy would, obviously, be in charge of the meeting but we would always have an input. That would lead to healthy arguments at times as we all had our opinions on tactics or team selections. Jimmy always had the final say as manager, but if

Jimmy Nicholl or I disagreed then he would know about it. We were open and honest and I think Jimmy Calderwood appreciated that. If it went to a vote then normally the 2–1 majority would win. One of the reasons why Jimmy Calderwood has been a top manager and we have been successful as a team is because Jimmy always listens closely and is willing to consider new things.

As well as being Jimmy Calderwood's first-team coach, I was his part-time minder on occasion. Like on Saturday, 7 January 2006 when we put Dundee United out of the Scottish Cup in the third round at Tannadice. Gordon Chisholm was manager of Dundee United and Billy Dodds was one of his coaches. They had been 2–0 up and ended up losing 3–2 so it was, obviously, a sore one for them to take. United had been struggling and were hurting after going out in the manner they did. The United camp were sick at the final whistle and we were just delighted to have scraped through.

We were walking down the side of track towards the tunnel when Billy turned and made a comment to Jimmy Calderwood about our previous meeting. It was needless and completely irrelevant. Jimmy didn't say anything. Billy then had another go and Jimmy finally took the bait. I was in the middle of them but Jimmy is a big man, as you know. I had him in my left hand and Billy in my right, to keep him away. Let me just say I had to use a bit of force to keep them apart.

I thought I had done a decent job but still ended up getting charged by the Scottish Football Association for my conduct. The charge was later dropped because their own investigations showed that I had only been trying to defuse the situation. The referee, Stuart Dougal, pulled us all in after the game and told us he had to take action or else the police were going to charge us all. Billy got a two-match ban while Jimmy and I both appealed. I was cleared, and rightly so, although Jimmy got fined and hit with a touchline ban. I always tell Jimmy my gift of the gab is better than his and that day in front of the SFA's disciplinary committee proved that!

But all joking aside Jimmy Calderwood is a top-drawer manager. I find it amazing that he has gone so long without getting another top job. I know he had that short spell at Ross County but I don't know why he hasn't landed another big job in Scotland or England. I just find it strange, especially when you see guys like Owen Coyle, Billy Davies and Derek McInnes who have all done well for themselves in England. They have all done brilliantly down south but if you look at their records in Scotland then they are nowhere near as good as Jimmy Calderwood's – taking Dunfermline into the SPL, Europe and to cup finals and then guiding Aberdeen into the top six every season he was at Pittodrie. For me, Jimmy's record speaks for itself. I am just amazed that nobody has given him another opportunity, yet.

32

THROUGH THE MILL AT ABERDEEN

TO THIS day I still don't know the exact reason why Jimmy Calderwood, Jimmy Nicholl and myself were sacked by Aberdeen at the end of the 2008–09 season. We had, once again, finished on a high by beating Hibs to claim a Europa League spot, but we knew before that final game that the axe was going to fall. We found out three or four days before that it was going to be our last match in charge. The players didn't know, only a handful of people were in the loop. We felt it was right to keep things quiet because the most important thing was to keep the players and the team focused on getting a result, one that might put Aberdeen back into Europe. We were desperate to qualify for the Europa League and to leave on a high, with our heads held high, and that is exactly what we did.

People were astonished when it was announced that we had parted company with Aberdeen. I know Jimmy loved his time at Aberdeen, we all did, and I think we all wish we could have had a bit longer at it, but that decision was taken out of our hands. Again it goes back to the questions, why and who was responsible for it?

I don't understand why the Aberdeen chairman, Stewart Milne, made the decision he did. I didn't, and still can't, see how dispensing with Jimmy Calderwood was in the best interests of

Aberdeen Football Club. Jimmy has had the best record of any Aberdeen manager in recent times. Every season he was at Pittodrie he guided his team into the top six, whereas his predecessors, Steve Paterson and Ebbe Skovdahl, struggled to survive in the SPL, never mind push for Europe.

I don't even know if Jimmy Calderwood is 100 percent certain as to the reasons why we are no longer at Pittodrie. We were told that it was a board decision and they wanted to take the club in another direction. I know Jimmy pushed a bit at the end to find out what was going to happen the following season, what direction we were going, the plans and the budget he would have available to him. In the end all these questions were irrelevant.

What I would say is that come the end of our time at Aberdeen there was very much a split on the football side. There was the two Jimmys and me on one side and Willie Miller, who was the then director of football, on the other. There wasn't much of a rapport on either side and the relationship between Jimmy Calderwood and Willie certainly wasn't like it was when he had first arrived at Pittodrie from Dunfermline in 2004.

The simple truth is we didn't need Willie Miller there. There was no need for Aberdeen to employ a director of football, whether it was Willie or anybody else. The two Jimmys and I all had decent contacts when it came to getting players in or on loan, as we showed by bringing in guys like Sone Aluko, Josh Walker and Javan Vidal. I think between us we had all the bases covered, especially when it came to the English game.

It wasn't as if Willie was really dealing with the financial aspect of the deals either because they were mainly done by the chief executive Duncan Fraser or David Johnston. Also we had Lenny Taylor, who was in charge of the youth set-up at Pittodrie, so, for me, there was no need to have Willie or any director of football at the club. We could have easily operated without one and in the final season we pretty much did. We hardly consulted with Willie at all. We kept everything in-house between ourselves, like the players we wanted and who we were keen to move on. We knew what direction we were going in, but, obviously, the Pittodrie hierarchy didn't share our vision for the future.

Another sore point for Jimmy and ourselves was Willie's decision to bring in Craig Robertson as chief scout. Craig was scouting players but wasn't working for the manager. How often does that happen at football clubs? I know that appointment really annoyed Jimmy and it is fair to say that Craig had absolutely no input or contact with any of the management when it came to targeting players. He was, obviously, working on a different agenda with Willie Miller. The reasons for that only Willie can answer.

People have to look closely at why Jimmy Calderwood was forced out. You could easily blame the chairman because he makes the final decision but how much was he influenced by other people? That is what we don't know. The day-to-day running of the club was left to Duncan Fraser and Willie Miller. It is quite clear that somebody stuck the knife into us, for reasons only known to themselves. I don't have any grievances with Duncan. He is a financial administrator and doesn't really know football outwith being a fan. I don't blame him for putting obstacles in our way but I really would love to know the part Willie Miller played in pushing us out the door. He knows how football works and when things are good or bad. In my opinion, and it is only a personal viewpoint, Willie no longer wanted to work with Jimmy Calderwood and that meant we all had to go.

If I am being honest, I have never really have had much of a relationship with Willie Miller and that goes back to when I was at Hearts and Walter Kidd got sent off in the 1986 Scottish Cup final. My memory of the next season was that when it came to the Aberdeen games I would always have a go at Willie physically on the pitch because of what he had done at Hampden. Time goes by and it was no longer an issue, although I never really saw eye-to-eye with him. There was no doubt there was also a major breakdown in his relationship with Jimmy. I know who I would have backed but the chairman, obviously, thought it would be easier to move his management team on than an Aberdeen legend.

Those last few weeks at Pittodrie were difficult but I have to say that one man, David Johnston, was magnificent throughout it all. 'DJ' was the go-between between the board and the management team and is one of the most professional people I have come across in football. As a player he wasn't the best but he was whole-hearted. He was a delight to work for as an administrator and unbelievably supportive of the football side. After the last game at Hibs, I remember Davie said to us, 'Well done for being so professional and for signing off the way you have.'

One of the reasons I later heard about our dismissal was that Jimmy was reluctant to give youth a chance. That is a load of garbage. Nobody needs to tell me the importance of bringing through your own young players. I did it at Hearts, Hamilton and St Johnstone. I am also aware of the problems a club can face if you don't produce your own talent.

The quality was certainly at Pittodrie and it was starting to come through. We had Peter Pawlett, Michael Paton and Chris Maguire, who all got an opportunity under Jimmy, while we also took Josh Walker, Sone Aluko and Javan Vidal on loan from English Premier League clubs, so it is absolute rubbish to say Jimmy wouldn't give youth a chance. Also, if we had still been there, then young boys like Fraser Fyvie, Ryan Jack and Mitch Megginson would have been given their opportunity.

Jimmy Calderwood, Jimmy Nicholl and myself all had a handle on who was coming through the youth ranks. We knew we had a good crop of youngsters and given time they would push into the first team. Credit must go to Lenny Taylor who used to head the youth set-up at Aberdeen. He did an absolutely tremendous job for the club. I know other people wanted to jump on the bandwagon and take credit for boys like Ryan Jack, Fraser Fyvie and Peter Pawlett but the men who were responsible for them coming through were Lenny Taylor and his staff.

To me, Willie was more a figurehead at Aberdeen than anything else. Willie has a magnificent standing at Pittodrie, going back to his playing days and rightly so because he has been a tremendous servant to Aberdeen. It was good for Aberdeen to have Willie in a PR sense but what he did at the club at the end of our tenure there, I am not exactly sure.

Don't get me wrong, outwith our issues with Willie everybody else at the club was different class and I would say it was up there with my time as a player with Hearts. The chairman Stewart Milne was always friendly and welcoming and I don't think there were too many times, when it came to looking for more money for players, where he turned Jimmy down. Obviously, there were budgets and we couldn't go much over them but, as a chairman, he was certainly very supportive.

I know our successor, Mark McGhee, had a go at everybody at the club after he left, from the office staff to the groundsman, but I couldn't talk more highly of everybody at Pittodrie. We were all one big, happy family and that was one of the reasons behind our success on the pitch.

I moved up to Aberdeen after Jimmy Calderwood and Jimmy Nicholl's first season at Pittodrie in 2005. Jimmy, to his credit, kept chipping away and managed to get me up. I ended up spending four great years in the Granite City and I have to say

I really enjoyed every single day of my four years up there. Aberdeen were always a club I had a lot of respect for, going all the way back when I was at Airdrie and Sir Alex Ferguson tried to sign me. I didn't get to Aberdeen as a player but I, at least, made it as a coach and it was a move that I will never have any regrets over.

There were so many highs. We always made the top six and there was also our UEFA Cup run of 2007–08. We beat Dnipro, who were as good as any side I have come across. We drew 0–0 at home and then went through on away goals after a 1–1 draw in the Ukraine. Darren Mackie got our all-important goal. That was typical Darren because he always gave it the best he had. Our defending in the second half of that game was top drawer, and guys like Jamie Langfield, Michael Hart, Scott Severin and Andrew Considine threw themselves in front of everything to stop Dnipro from scoring.

It was incredibly emotional come the final whistle. We had achieved a tremendous feat, just to get into the group stages. There we met Atletico Madrid, Panathinaikos, Copenhagen and Lokomotiv Moscow. We really should have had no chance, but once again the boys dug deep and defied the odds by drawing with Lokomotiv and then thumping Copenhagen at Pittodrie to see us progress in third spot. Our reward was that amazing draw against Bayern Munich.

The night the German giants visited Pittodrie was another special one, where our on-loan youngsters Sone Aluko and Josh Walker got our goals in a 2–2 draw. We put on a really spirited display before Bayern came out and showed their quality by beating us 5–1 in the Allianz Arena return, where we saw a real step up in class. Bayern were absolutely ruthless that night.

Over our time at Aberdeen we were lucky to have so many great players. If we had managed to keep most of them then I am pretty certain we could have been up there challenging the Old Firm for the SPL title. I am talking about players like Kevin McNaughton, Michael Hart, Chris Clark, Russell Anderson and Barry Nicholson. If we had kept them then I firmly believe we would have been in a real position of strength to battle with Rangers and Celtic. We really could have been a top force in Scottish football, but it wasn't to be. Needs must and some of them were sold while others left on freedom of contract, the lure and money down south proving too much of a pull for the boys, and who could blame them? It is a short career.

I didn't have a lot to do with the financial side of things but our budgets did become tighter and tighter. It would have been great to have kept our top players but it was never going to happen. When you lose players of that quality then it is near impossible to replace them. There were a lot of similarities to the end of my own time at St Johnstone, when we had less money and I tried to go out and buy experience. Jimmy signed Stevie Crawford at the tail end of his career because we knew he had quality. Craig Brewster was another one, along with the likes of Alan Maybury and Jackie McNamara. We signed older players to try and give us a balance and to use their experience to help bring the younger players at the club on.

The main disappointment from our time at Pittodrie was our cup record. It was poor and still remains a source of irritation to Jimmy Calderwood, Jimmy Nicholl and myself. We all knew the Aberdeen fans craved a cup final appearance and nothing would have given us greater pleasure to deliver, but, for a variety of reasons, it just didn't happen. When you analyse things closely we lost to Queen's Park in the 2006 League Cup, in a game we should have won but lost on penalties. That is not an excuse because great credit must go to Billy Stark and his players for the performance his Queen's team put on that night. We also lost to Dunfermline on penalties in the Scottish Cup but the worst of the lot was losing the Scottish Cup semi-final to Queen of the South at Hampden in 2008. It was unbelievable how poor we were on the day. The goals we lost and the way we defended were just criminal. If you go down to Hampden and score three goals then you should expect to win the game. The fact we lost 4–3 summed up how poorly we had played and that result was probably the biggest nail in our Pittodrie coffin.

To this day, outwith our cup record, I am pretty certain that Stewart Milne must regret his decision to terminate Jimmy Calderwood's contract. The club have only gone one way since then and that has been a downward spiral. The club replaced us with the Gothenburg legend Mark McGhee but after just over a season he was moved on and replaced by the Motherwell boss Craig Brown. Despite all the managerial changes the club have still got nowhere near the level they reached under Jimmy Calderwood. The statistics and his record speak for themselves.

33

STAG PARTIES, TRAINING-GROUND BUST-UPS AND TOUCHLINE TANTRUMS

I USED to go in on a Sunday and take the Aberdeen players who had been on the bench and hadn't played, along with the fringe boys, for training. I used to call them the 'Grumpy Squad', as they felt coming in on a Sunday was a punishment more than anything else. They could be a difficult group to handle because mentally and physically the boys weren't exactly at their peak. The majority of the time the boys would get their heads down and just get on with things, although you knew there was always potential for a flashpoint or two. That was what happened one morning when our experienced striker, Steve Lovell, decided to over-step the mark. He was a good player, who had made a name for himself at Dundee and Portsmouth, but he had a lot of bad luck with injuries at Pittodrie. It was unfortunate, for us and Steve, because if we had kept him fit and playing the way we knew he could then he would have been in the team every week. He was as quick as anybody around and also had an eye for a goal.

Stevie was in this particular Sunday and was clearly annoyed and unhappy that he hadn't been involved with the first team against Celtic the previous day. I took the training and set up a small-sided game. Steve lost the ball after he had been tackled by our young defender Scott Ross, Steve turned round and just booted him. There was no need for it and it was totally out of order. His actions completely infuriated me. I went mad and left him without a name. Things became pretty heated and he turned round and told me to f*** off. I came so close to punching him because he was well out of order. I could have quite easily swung at him but as a member of the management team I knew I had to show a bit of restraint and professionalism. Steve might have been frustrated, we have all been there, but to kick a young player who he knew was never going to kick him back was just cowardly. I remember I said to him, 'Why don't you kick me?' But he wasn't that stupid. I decided to let Jimmy Calderwood deal with Steve rather than take things into my own hands. Jimmy was far from impressed with Steve and decided to fine him. It cost Steve a wee bit of money, but hopefully he learned a valuable lesson from the whole sorry episode. For me, it probably summed Steve up – he could score, was lightning fast and had all the attributes to do really well but maybe lacked that bit of extra spark to really go places.

Steve wasn't the only one to fall foul of Mr Calderwood. Our goalkeeper, Jamie Langfield, was another player who almost shot himself in the foot, although that was more down to his off-the-field antics. We were on our annual Majorca trip at the end of the season, where the two Jimmys and I were out having a quiet beer. It was also Jamie's stag week and quite a few of the boys had come out, like Derek Young and Darren Mackie, to see out his final days as a single man. It was good to meet up with them and there was absolutely no hassle. The first time we bumped into Jamie and the boys we had a good few beers and it was a good laugh. Jamie started to get a little worse for wear the longer the night went on and a couple of times I had to pull him away from Jimmy Calderwood. He wasn't being nasty, more of a drunken pest. It went on and on and again I had to continue acting as peacemaker and drag him away from Jimmy, that was fine. Jimmy was a bit annoyed because of the state Jamie had got himself in but accepted it was his stag party and so, in the end, decided to turn a blind eye to things. There were no problems and everything passed peacefully, until the next evening.

We were outside the Bronze Bar in Magaluf, a local establishment that is popular with a lot of the football fraternity and is owned by my friend Bobby Drummond. It is our usual haunt for the Champions League final. When we arrived Jamie was already sitting, slumped, drunk and completely out of it. I am all for people having a drink and a good time but just don't do it in front of the wrong people or when your manager is there. I have to say it was embarrassing, the state Jamie was in. That along with the events of the previous evening sent Jimmy Calderwood over the edge and he lost the plot with Jamie.

Eventually some of Jamie's mates moved to defuse the situation and took him back to his hotel room, which was probably the best place for him. Jimmy was absolutely fuming after that and Jamie paid the price because he lost the No. 1 spot at the start of the new season. It was a harsh lesson but one I hope Jamie realises was for his own good.

Credit to him, he never threw in the towel. He put his hands up and apologised although I am certain he won't remember much of what he was saying sorry for. There was nothing outrageous but Jamie had just been a bit irresponsible and stupid, but that's goalkeepers for you. Jamie kept working away and eventually got himself back in the team. He became one of the strong characters in our dressing room and was one of the main voices for us in our final season. As a goalkeeper and a person he was first class and a real top performer. To be fair, at Aberdeen there were very few problems behind the scenes. We had a good bunch of lads who all wanted to do well for themselves, each other and the club.

Another major talking point from my time at Aberdeen was my on-going feud with the-then Hearts manager Csaba Laszlo or the Drama Queen as I used to call him. I didn't know the man before he came to Scotland and after my dealings with him I certainly hope that continues to be the case. He arrived at Hearts in 2008 and I first came across him when we travelled down to Tynecastle for a league game that October. We had gone ahead through a Darren Mackie goal although Lee Wallace equalised for Hearts. The game was pretty evenly poised and late on the referee, Steve Conroy, awarded Hearts a penalty when he adjudged that Jamie Langfield had brought down Michael Stewart. He pointed to the spot but after speaking to his assistant he reversed his decision. He had been told Stewart had dived and gave us a goal kick. Laszlo was absolutely fuming. To be fair, the referee got the decision spot on and television pictures later vindicated his actions. At the final whistle, Laszlo was up at Conroy and the officials, having a go at them. I tried to help him out and defuse the situation before he got himself into bother. I said to him, 'Just leave it. It isn't worth it. You will just get yourself into trouble.' He turned, looked at me as if I was dirt and brushed me away. It was such an ignorant thing to do and I really could have turned and smashed him. I was fuming. I had been trying to help him and he threw it back in my face. That was the start of my horrendous relationship with Mr Laszlo and his German assistant Werner Burger.

Burger, for me, was the one who supplied the bullets for Laszlo, who was out on the touchline trying to cause havoc and help his team gain any advantage they could. I know he caused problems and tensions with our bench but it wasn't just with Aberdeen. Talking to other people in football, Mr Laszlo certainly upset a lot of people in the game.

After every game we would always go to the home manager's

room for a drink – win, lose or draw. We went into the manager's office at Tynecastle after that game and waited for ten to fifteen minutes but Mr Laszlo never appeared. As far as I'm concerned, that just summed him up. After that we never went anywhere near his office again.

It got to the stage where I even refused to shake hands with Laszlo or Burger. I had no respect for either of them. Don't get me wrong, Laszlo had something to offer as a coach because he was relatively successful at Hearts, but the way he conducted himself was out of order. I didn't hate Laszlo or Burger as people but I disliked the way they acted. What annoyed me more was that I knew what an honour it was to manage a great club like Hearts. I had worked at Hearts under a great manager in Alex MacDonald. People had nothing but respect for the way Alex handled himself and represented the club. He was a figure people respected, like Jim Jefferies, who went on take over from Laszlo. Seeing Laszlo act the way he did I felt was embarrassing for him and Hearts.

His time at Tynecastle will hardly go down as one of the most exciting periods in the club's history. I have never seen so many Hearts players dive and fall down as often as I did when I watched Laszlo's sides. I am talking about big strong guys, over six feet, who would go down with the slightest contact like they had been shot. Laszlo's teams adopted tactics that are widespread in European football, but these are things the Scottish game is a lot better without.

The next time we faced them was at Pittodrie a couple of months later. We beat them 1–0. Marius Zaliukas was sent off during the game and Lee Wallace was also red-carded after having a go at the referee, Iain Brines. Everything looked to have settled down until we got into the tunnel and Robbie Neilson completely lost the plot. Robbie is a really nice guy and somebody I have a lot of respect for but that afternoon he just saw red and starting swinging punches at Lee Mair and Chris Maguire. He kicked things off and then disappeared into the away dressing room, sparking a real fracas. I found myself in the middle of things trying to act as peacemaker. I was then confronted by the Hearts striker Christian Nade, who is some size. If he had shown the same aggression he did in the tunnel that day out on the pitch then he would have been some player. Eventually both sides were calmed down without much damage being done. That, however, summed up Laszlo and his team. Maybe if they had shown as much fight on the pitch then they might have taken a few more points under Mr Laszlo.

34

SHREDDING THE NERVES AT
KILMARNOCK

KILMARNOCK WAS a strange one for us from the start. Jimmy Calderwood almost blew the job before we had actually got it. I took a phone call, from the co-author of this book strangely enough, to see if Jimmy would be interested in the Rugby Park post. It was just as Kilmarnock were in the process of finalising the settlement agreements of their management team, Jim Jefferies and Billy Brown. I spoke to Jimmy and right away he said he would be, knowing Kilmarnock were a good club. That information was then relayed to the Rugby Park hierarchy, although no contact was made with Jimmy until after Jefferies and Brown had left Rugby Park. The Kilmarnock chairman, Michael Johnston, then called Jimmy, but before that happened Jimmy did a bit of work for BBC Radio.

There had been a bit of speculation linking Jimmy with the Kilmarnock job and he was asked about the situation. Jimmy went on air and said he had been sounded out about the job a couple of days earlier, the day before Jim Jefferies and Billy Brown actually left the club. He made it sound like he had been approached by Kilmarnock. I remember it caused a bit of a furore on the radio, with people thinking he had been lined up for the post before Jim and Billy had actually left. That wasn't the case. Jimmy had been sounded out, by me, but there had been absolutely no contact with Kilmarnock. Everything was eventually finalised with Jimmy and Billy and then Kilmarnock appointed Jimmy Calderwood as their new manager, with Jimmy Nicholl as his assistant. Both agreed short-term deals until the end of the season. Budgets were tight and it was a week later before I joined them at Rugby Park.

Kilmarnock were struggling at the bottom end of the league. Jim Jefferies and Billy Brown both did an excellent job at Killie but, by their own admission, they had probably been there too long and should have moved on earlier. When you look at Jim and Billy's record, throughout their managerial careers at Falkirk, Hearts and Kilmarnock, they certainly stand up there with the best. I wouldn't criticise them for one minute although when we arrived at Rugby Park there was a wee bit of staleness about the place and it took a real effort to try and change that.

There was also very little time or money to change things. We were at the end of the transfer window and most of the wage budget was accounted for. The players had been used to working in certain ways and, for me, there were one or two little cliques amongst the players. It took a real effort to bring everybody that wee bit closer together. We made a couple of decent additions in the transfer market by bringing in our former players Scott Severin and Chris Maguire on loan, and they gave us a bit of a lift. Wee Chris scored the winner early on against Celtic and at that point we thought it was going to be onwards and upwards. We had some good performances but there were also some indifferent ones, shall we say. At times, there seemed to be a bit of softness about the squad. It was a real battle to keep away from relegation. We would win games but we would never be able to drag ourselves away from trouble. In the final week we had to go to our old stomping ground of Pittodrie, needing to get a result. It is bizarre how these little quirks of fate turn up in football. Fortunately, we went up there and Kevin Kyle scored a really good header to win us the game.

It put our destiny back in our own hands, going into that last game of the season at home to Falkirk, who were bottom of the table. We knew that as long as we didn't lose then we would remain in the SPL.

That last day was a real nail-biter. I wouldn't like to go through too many afternoons like that in my career. The game, not surprisingly, was a nervy affair and could have gone either way. I thought we looked reasonably comfortable and never really looked like losing it, although you always know that one lucky break or counter attack and you could be in the mire. I remember the young Falkirk player, Ryan Flynn, had a wee half-chance that he put just over the bar. If that had gone in then we would have been in a very alarming situation. That is how close these types of situations can be, you really are on a knife-edge. Fortunately for us, and unfortunately for Falkirk, we managed to see it through. It was a relief for everyone at the club, knowing Kilmarnock's financial situation. I hate to think what might have happened if the club had dropped into the First Division.

It had been a tough few final weeks and at the end of the season all the management team headed off to Spain for a break to recharge the batteries. We didn't know if we were staying at Kilmarnock or not because our contracts were up. We continued as if we were going to stay on and started to make plans to strengthen the squad. The club were looking to tighten their belts and, in the end, the chairman eventually came back to Jimmy and made a pretty derisory offer to keep him and his staff. I think that was the chairman's way of saying he wanted to go in another direction. I spoke to Jimmy and said that I would walk away if there was enough money for him and Jimmy Nicholl to take things on again. They didn't and I don't think the chairman had any real intentions of keeping them. I think Jimmy himself sensed that. It was strange because early on, around the January, February and March of that previous season, the chairman had been desperate to get us all to sign new contracts but then, obviously, he had a change of heart. I think the chairman could certainly have handled things better. He could have just come out and said thanks for what you have done. We could all have moved on – without the pantomime and the way it all ended. I am certain that if we had remained we could have made Kilmarnock a major force again, but it wasn't to be.

The club eventually went for Mixu Paatelainen and Kenny Shiels, and, to be fair, they have gone from strength to strength since then, winning the Scottish League Cup in 2012. Mr Johnston will feel he has been vindicated.

35

THE BEEB, BERTI VOGTS, SUTTON
AND THE ROAD TO SEVILLE

OVER THE last twenty years, on and off due to my club commitments, I have been lucky enough to work with the BBC, whether it be on television or radio. When I was still at Hearts I was initially asked to go and do some co-commentary work and I have to say it was something I enjoyed from the off. The BBC kept asking me back, so I must have done something right somewhere. I have always enjoyed watching football and in the periods where I have been out of the game the BBC have continued to give me work and to keep me involved. It has worked well for me and hopefully it has worked just as well for the 'Beeb' over the years.

When the BBC had the live games on the television I did the summarising and co-commentary with Rob McLean. I was fortunate that Tom Connor, who was in charge of television for BBC Sport Scotland, gave me that opportunity. Rob is a top commentator and both he and I were able to work away at things. I felt we built up a really good rapport. I thoroughly enjoyed doing it and the feedback from the punters was good.

Doing the live games on television is always good but at times you know that it can be like flying without a safety harness. You can make mistakes or be left red-faced, which has happened to me on occasion. It certainly did on 11 August 2002 when I was doing the Edinburgh derby at Tynecastle. It was the game where Hearts thrashed Hibs 5–1. Hearts were winning 3–1 and Mark de Vries had scored a couple of the goals. Rob McLean and I were doing the commentary when he turned to me and said, 'Sandy, can you give us a man of the match?' De Vries had scored a couple but I still felt Jean-Louis Valois, who had played down the left, had been different class and so I gave the award to him. Then in stoppage time De Vries scored another two goals to take his tally to four. By that time, I had already given Valois the vote and there was no going back. Needless to say, I took a lot of good-bantered stick for not giving De Vries the decision, as he had walked away with the match ball, four goals and the scalp of Hibs. If only I had a crystal ball then I might have made a different choice!

Another famous one, which is probably one of my Colemanballs, came on a European night when I was covering a Celtic game. Rob turned and said, 'John Hartson is playing superbly today.' My response was 'Yes, Rob, there's no one better today.' That was fine until Rob turned again and asked, 'So Sandy, who is your man of the match?' Quick as a flash I said, 'Alan Thompson.' I had spent the previous twenty seconds agreeing with Rob that Hartson had been the best player on the pitch and then I went with Thompson. It was one David Coleman would have been proud of. Live television can expose you to these sorts of things, you have to think on your feet and keep your wits about you. I was going to explain that Thompson had been right up there with Hartson but the action kicked in again and I didn't get that opportunity.

Celtic did quite well in Europe under Martin O'Neill during that time, so I covered quite a few of their games, especially the 2002–03 season when they made the UEFA Cup final. I was normally working elsewhere and so I waited until the last minute to fly out to the matches and then I would fly back the morning after. The problem was that when it came to Celtic games the BBC used to put us on supporters' flights. That was fine although being a former Rangers player didn't exactly help my cause in those situations. There is always a good bit of banter with a lot of the fans, which is always good natured although at times there is the occasional situation where things could boil over. That happened on our way back from Celtic's game with Celta Vigo in December of 2002. Circumstances at the airport that night didn't help either.

The police had been completely over the top and had started on the Celtic support after a couple of fans had dropped some beer bottles. They just waded into the Celtic fans and a supporter in a wheelchair got attacked. It was just disgraceful and the whole place was on edge.

There was a fan who spotted me and started to mouth off, spouting all the usual bigoted rubbish, mainly because I was an ex-Rangers player. He was trying to get to me but the rest of the BBC travelling party and the Celtic supporters round us were great and kept him away. The nearer we got to the gate the closer he got to me and at one stage I thought I was going to have to swing for him. I already had my fist clenched. If it was going to kick off then I was going to get in first because I had no idea what this guy was capable of, not because I wanted to. I thought I was going to have to defend myself. In the end, I managed to push through the gate and that calmed what could have been a tricky situation. Otherwise, I don't know what would have happened. If I had punched this idiot then I don't know how the rest of the Celtic fans would have reacted, especially after everything that had happened beforehand with the police. Celtic lost 2–1 but went through on away goals, so, at least there was one silver lining from that night.

I have to say after that incident I feared the worst when the BBC told me I was going out to Seville to cover the UEFA Cup final. There was expected to be more than 80,000 Celtic fans in the Spanish city. That was going to be a challenge for a former Rangers player. We were to be out in Seville for four or five days and so it was going to be a wee bit difficult to go for a beer or a quiet meal without getting into one or two discussions with Celtic fans. Chick Young was with us and he is almost as popular with the Celtic support as me. One of his pals, Tommy Nolan, had his own boat, the *Carbon Copy*, and had sailed up the River Guadalquivir for the game. We managed to escape for a day and sailed up and down the river, having a few beers and a really good day. Elaine C. Smith and her husband were also on the boat and it was certainly different from how I had passed time at other European games.

I have covered hundreds of games for the BBC, all over the country and Europe. It has been a pleasure doing so many big games and watching so many top players and teams. One of the big matches I covered was the final day of the 2002–03 season. Rangers and Celtic were both going for the title and my old club went into that last match one goal better off than their city rivals. Celtic were at Kilmarnock, while Rangers were at home to Dunfermline, and I was covering the game at Ibrox on Sunday, 23 May 2003.

Rangers eventually beat Dunfermline 6–1 to win the league and that led to the Celtic striker Chris Sutton accusing the Dunfermline players of lying down. Having been at the game I am in no doubt that was not the case. Dunfermline actually played really well, strange as it seems when you look at the final score-line. They took the game back to 1–1 and the Rangers goalkeeper Stefan Klos had two or three outstanding saves to keep Dunfermline at bay. Jimmy Calderwood and Jimmy Nicholl got a bit of stick after that game for the result but if you were a neutral watching the match you would have seen their team was absolutely committed that day. I went to work with Dunfermline the next season and I found that about a third of that team were actually Celtic fans. Mark McGarty, who gave away the penalty for Mikel Arteta's goal for the sixth goal, was also a massive Celtic fan. Nobody can tell me he wanted Rangers to win the league.

It doesn't matter who you support because when you wear somebody else's jersey you should always give 100 percent for that team. When you look at these things and the people who were involved I am in no doubt that Chris Sutton was totally wrong with his comments. His accusations were well wide of the mark. I know he apologised and I am sure he will still be embarrassed when he looks back on his comments. I am sure it was nothing but hurt and frustration on Chris's part and I know how he felt. I harboured similar disappointments when I lost the league with Hearts on the last day of the 1985–85. The only reason I knew that some of the St Mirren team hadn't all given 100 percent was because one of their players told me. I know after going on to work with the Dunfermline boys the next season they would never have thrown a game or laid down for anybody. Chris's comments certainly hurt the Dunfermline boys and maybe in future Celtic games they came back to haunt him.

I have been a player and a manager and I know how tough it can be. It is easy to criticise and put the boot in but I have always tried to be balanced with my views and opinions. The one guy I did give more than a fair bit of stick to was Berti Vogts, as his time in charge of Scotland was horrendous. The damage he did our game was unbelievable.

I was down covering the friendly when Wales hammered us 4–0 in the Millennium Stadium back in February 2004. We got absolutely thrashed and the Scotland team that night was an absolute shambles. It was embarrassing to say you were a Scot that night and I was delighted to see the back of Berti not long after that. His appointment was a massive mistake but thankfully the Scottish Football Associaton got things right with Walter Smith, Alex McLeish and now Craig Levein. We are now in good safe hands with my former Hearts captain and teammate. It at least makes Scotland's matches that bit more enjoyable to cover.

I have come across so many good people at the BBC. Rob McLean is a first-class commentator and David Begg, without a shadow of doubt, is the best radio commentator in the business. They are both experienced, top professionals. John 'Digger' Barnes is another good operator and when you talk about the BBC you can't ignore Chick Young. I used to love covering Celtic games with him because, as a 'St Mirren fan', he would always take some of the flak away from me. When you went away with Chick you knew you were going to get a good night out. He is just really good, enjoyable company.

I used to do the Saturday afternoon show on the radio where I had many a run-in with my old Airdrie pal Jim Traynor. A lot of people were a bit scared of him but we went back a long way and I always got in about him, which was good fun. Behind the scenes, there are people like Tom Connor and Claire Kelly who also do a lot of good work that always goes unnoticed. I have known them, and worked with them, for a long time and they have been great and really supportive to me throughout the years.

36

A FURTHER EDUCATION

I STILL work regularly with the BBC and manage to fit it round my work as a lecturer at Cumbernauld College. I can imagine a few of you are now raising your eyebrows having already learned about my school qualifications. Let's just say I am better qualified now than when I was back then.

I am lecturing at the college and that came about through my SFA coaching commitments where I was helping to do the A Licence down at Largs. I have done that for a few years now and put a number of top managers and coaches through their paces, from Gary McAllister to Colin Calderwood, Ian Durrant and John Hughes. Lately Stephen McManus and John Kennedy have done the course. It is also funny because I have helped many of my former players, like Paul Ritchie, Grant Murray, Allan Johnston and Scott Leitch, take the next step on their coaching careers. It seems like only yesterday they were still playing.

Another one of my graduates was a Spanish coach called Pedro Marques. I put him through his paces on the A Licence. He went on to work for Manchester City and was the guy who was seen trying to talk Carlos Tevez off the bench the night he refused to take to the field in that infamous Champions League game against Bayern Munich. I certainly hope my explanations were better than Pedro's that night.

There are a lot of people in football who love to have a go at the so-called 'Largs Mafia'. I have to say there are very few more professional organisations; the coaching courses on offer from the SFA are more highly thought of than the English Football Association. Up here you are allowed to express yourself any way you want and that for me is how it should be done. That is why guys like Jose Mourinho and Andre Villas-Boas did some of their badges through the SFA. It shows that Jim Fleeting and all the boys down there must be doing something right.

As mentioned earlier, it was thanks to my involvement with the A Licence coaching course that I got my job with Cumbernauld College. Todd Lumsden, who was a player-coach at Albion Rovers at the time, was on the course back in 2010. Two or three weeks later Todd phoned me and said that he helped run a course at the college and they were on the lookout for a lecturer to run their football course. I knew a bit about it because my old Hearts team-mate Allan Moore had been involved before he left to become manager of Morton.

I had reservations and told Todd that. I was a football coach but when it came to the other side of things I would struggle to even spell lecturer, but he convinced me to go and have a chat with the principal, Martin McGuire. We had a good discussion and I explained how I felt young players should be developed and brought on. Things went well and Martin was pleased with what he had heard and offered me the job, despite my concerns. He then told me that if he wanted to run a course on bricklaying then he would need to employ a 'brickie' and it was the same when it came to football. He said I would have no problems lecturing and I could learn as I went.

I have since got to know Martin fairly well. He is very professional at his job and he has a real passion for the game and the development of young football talent. He is very supportive to everyone in the sports department.

The college runs two courses, a football course for youngsters who are leaving school and a rugby course. Both are run along similar lines and are based at Broadwood Stadium and feel more like a professional sports club than a college set-up. I get great enjoyment from working with Todd and the rest of the guys. Another member of the team is the ex-Celtic manager and player Davie Hay, who I didn't really know until we started to work together but I have really enjoyed our times together reminiscing about our playing days.

My other colleagues in the sports department include Jamie Dempsey, who also coaches in the second tier of Scottish rugby, and there is Davie Mitchell, Ally Breton and Sean Tough. I have been amazed at the amount of sports science knowledge that these guys have and I have picked up a lot of fresh ideas and techniques from them. Hopefully it has been a two-way street.

We have quite a few students who are also involved with Dumbarton, Clyde, Raith Rovers and Stirling Albion. We have a strong tie with the SFA and quite often they will use the boys for their coaching courses and games. It has been a win-win situation for everyone involved, from the students to the college and myself. Hopefully my own experiences throughout my football career help the students with their future career plans – in or outwith the game. Both the rugby and football courses have certainly given a lot to many young people coming through the ranks and I am sure ties with senior clubs will continue to flourish.

It is great to still be involved in football after all these years. The game has been a massive part of my life and I can look back on my time in football with great pride. I have had a lot of enjoyment from the game I love. It was a dream come true from day one when I signed for my boyhood team Airdrie. I then went on to captain the Diamonds and help them make their mark in Scotland's top flight. Helping Airdrie to win promotion and then being named as the Scottish Players' Player of the Year were two massive things for me. If I am being honest, my time at Broomfield probably went better than even I could have imagined. The only disappointment was that the club were relegated from the Scottish Premier Division just before I left. I would have loved to have kept Airdrie up but it wasn't to be. That is my only real regret from my time at Airdrie.

Moving on to West Ham United was another massive thing for me. I had always wanted to play in England and to get the chance to play with a top club like the Hammers was amazing. It was great playing with and against some of the biggest players and characters in the British game. I thought I did reasonably well in my short time at Upton Park and, as I said earlier, maybe with hindsight I should have stuck it out a bit longer in England.

I was maybe a bit hasty in returning to Scotland, but then again when a club like Rangers comes calling it is quite often a case of now or never. It was a great experience playing for Rangers. I also managed to lift the Skol Cup but the one negative from my time there was that we never won the league, or really got close to it during my spell at Ibrox.

Hearts is probably where I will be best remembered. I loved my time at Tynecastle as a player and manager and I still have a great rapport with the Hearts fans and I only wish we had been able to reward them with a trophy. I am grateful to Wallace Mercer for giving me my big break in management. I would have loved to have finished the job I started but unfortunately the sale of the club meant it wasn't to be. The way I was sacked did hurt me but it will never change my feelings for the club and the supporters.

I also had some successful spells in management with Hamilton and St Johnstone. Winning promotion with Accies was great while finishing third, getting to a cup final and leading St Johnstone back into Europe was also massive. I think my managerial record stands up pretty well. It was unfortunate how my time at McDiarmid Park came to an end but, as I have said, I believe there were a lot of circumstances that were outwith my control.

I also had some good times with Jimmy Calderwood and Jimmy Nicholl at Aberdeen, Dunfermline and Kilmarnock. We had a lot of good times together and at every club we had some form of success.

Throughout my life and my career I have always given 100 percent. I think all the fans appreciated my efforts and that is why I have always had a close bond with so many supporters of my former clubs. I think they know that whenever I have worn their jersey or put on their coaching or managerial jacket, I have been honest and given absolutely everything I have.

I have been out of the dugout for a couple of seasons now. But I have still been keeping my hand in with my media work and my job at Cumbernauld College. As for the future, I am thoroughly enjoying my time as a lecturer but I still feel I have something to offer within the professional game – at whatever level remains to be seen. I hope there is still another chapter or two to write.

SANDY CLARK'S CAREER STATS

PLAYING CAREER

	APPEARANCES	GOALS
AIRDRIE (1974–82)		
1974–75	1 (2)	
1975–76	19 (2)	7
1976–77	31 (8)	10
1977–78	39 (1)	7
1978–79	44	26
1979–80	40	23
1980–81	43	11
1981–82	37	17
WEST HAM UNITED (1982–83)		
1982–83	34	10
RANGERS (1983–84)		
1982–83	13	7
1983–84	39 (6)	15
1984–85	3	

HEARTS (1984–89)

1984–85	30	5
1985–86	40	7
1986–87	51	10
1987–88	15 (25)	5
1988–89	3 (1)	1

PARTICK THISTLE (1989–90 PLAYER-MANAGER)

1989–90	1 (2)

DUNFERMLINE ATHLETIC (1989–90)

1989–90	3 (1)

CAREER ACHIEVEMENTS

AIRDRIE – Named as the Scottish Professional Footballers' Association Player of the Year in 1981–82

RANGERS – League Cup Winner in 1983–84

MANAGERIAL/COACHING CAREER

HEARTS
1988–89 – Reserve/youth team coach at Hearts

PARTICK THISTLE (1989–90)
1989–90 – Appointed manager. Finished 8th in the First Division

HEARTS (1990-94)
1990–93 – Reserve/youth team coach at Hearts
1993–94 – Appointed manager. Finished 7th in the Scottish Premier Division

HAMILTON ACCIES (1994–98)

1994–95 – Appointed commercial manager/no. 2 with Hamilton

1996 – Named as Hamilton manager

1996–97 – Led Hamilton to promotion for the Scottish Second Division

ST JOHNSTONE (1998–2001)

Appointed manager of St Johnstone

1998–99 – Led Saints to third spot in the Scottish Premier League, the CIS Cup Final and back into Europe

DUNFERMLINE ATHLETIC (2003–04)

First-team coach at Dunfermline

BERWICK RANGERS (2004–05)

Named manager of Berwick Rangers

ABERDEEN (2005–09)

First-team coach at Aberdeen

KILMARNOCK (2009–10)

First-team coach at Kilmarnock

MANAGERIAL ACHIEVEMENTS

HEARTS – Led Hearts to the under-19 Scottish Cup

HAMILTON – Named the Second Division Manager of the Year in 1996–97